W0082724

# MILL VILLAGERS AND FARMERS: DIALECT AND ECONOMICS IN A SMALL SOUTHERN TOWN

# MILL VILLAGERS AND FARMERS: DIALECT AND ECONOMICS IN A SMALL SOUTHERN TOWN

ELIZABETH DuPREE McNAIR

*Virginia Polytechnic Institute and State University*

Publication of the American Dialect Society

•

Number 90

•

*Published by Duke University Press for the American Dialect Society*

*Annual Supplement to* American Speech

PUBLICATION OF THE AMERICAN DIALECT SOCIETY

RONALD R. BUTTERS, Editor, *Duke University*
CHARLES E. CARSON, Managing Editor, *Duke University*

Number 90
Copyright © 2005
American Dialect Society
ISBN: 0-8223-6622-3

Library of Congress Cataloging-in-Publication Data

McNair, Elizabeth DuPree
Mill villagers and farmers : dialect and economics in a small southern town / Elizabeth DuPree McNair
p. cm. — (Publication of the American Dialect Society ; no. 90)
"Annual supplement to American Speech"
Includes bibliographical references
ISBN 0-8223-6622-3 (cloth : alk. paper)
1. English language—Dialects—Georgia—Griffin. 2. Griffin (Ga.)—Economic conditions. 3. Americanisms—Georgia—Griffin. 4. Griffin (Ga.)—Social conditions. I. American Dialect Society. II. American speech. III. Title. IV. Series.
PE3101.G4M37 2005
427'.9758443–dc22 2005023604

British Library Cataloguing-in-Publication Data available

# CONTENTS

# 1. A SOCIOLINGUISTIC STUDY OF A SOUTHERN MILL TOWN

This is a report on a sociolinguistic study of dialect change in Griffin, Georgia, a textile mill town about 40 miles south of Atlanta (see figure 1.1). Local dialects are patterning, in the context of "cultural contours" (Kurath 1949; Pederson 1986–92), in two groups of the working class: the mill workers and the farmers. However, it is also true, as Bailey (1997) claims, that some current stereotypical features of American Southern White Vernacular Englishes (SWVE) probably developed recently and do not still reflect original settlement patterns as Kurath claimed.

Griffin, the seat of Spalding County, was originally inhabited by Creek Indians who managed to survive waves of conquerors from the 1540s until 1823. After that point, pioneers settled the land by giving away small (202.5-acre) plots of land in a lottery, and cotton became the main crop. The first significant period of growth, in the early 1840s, coincided with the building of the Monroe Railroad, owned by General Lewis Lawrence Griffin. This north-south line enabled farmers to transport goods to more markets. General Griffin also planned an east-west line, but the Depression of 1843 halted construction and this line was later extended to Terminus (Atlanta) instead. In the 1880s, the Kincaid Manufacturing Company opened the first textile mill in Griffin. This industry continued to expand and became Griffin's largest employer in the early twentieth century. Griffin's population today is about 22,000 and, although the textile industry has declined, population is growing due to its new status as a "bedroom community" to Atlanta.

## THEORY AND DATA

The purpose of this study is to record dialectal variation in two dialect communities in Griffin and to observe change through apparent time. In addition to this traditional stratificational approach, these speech communities are investigated as products of specific

FIGURE 1.1
Location of Griffin, Georgia

sociocultural processes. While one goal is to systematically record variable speech patterns in Griffin, it is equally important to analyze these data with respect to how speakers interact and shape language use (Gumperz 1972; Milroy 1987b). The experimental method of analysis used here involves data collection through interviews that provide examples of vernacular speech along with information enabling a construction of each speaker's social network. In addition to providing a valuable data point for the ongoing research on North American varieties of English, this study also addresses the theoretical goal of correlating social behavior and socioeconomic patterns with linguistic change.

Two groups in Griffin, farmers and mill villagers, are observed as once-separate speech communities, each constituting a "field of action where distribution of linguistic variants is a reflection of social facts" (Gumperz 1972, 225). By observing their co-occurrence with factors such as migration, occupation, age, sex, and social network, speech variants can be seen as "indices of social patterns of interaction in the speech community" (221). The two communities each embody a different "locality" in Silverstein's (1998, 404) application of the term—that is, not necessarily referring to physical geography but rather to an "ethnographic and ethnohistorical sense of community boundedness about a 'center' that constitutes locality as a cultural fact." The centering institution in these groups has been largely socioeconomic, the mill villagers grouped around the textile mill establishment, and the farmers grouped around the local industry of producing and selling cotton. In other words, these people may be found to have a "contrastive and positive sense of their participation in their own language community" that implies "groupness" (404–5). As contact between these communities has increased over the past century, patterns of cross-cultural diffusion have developed. This contact ecology entails an expanded pool of features, providing more linguistic options to individual speakers (J. Milroy 1992; Mufwene 1999), and an interesting example of how socioeconomic trends affect social behavior and thus language change.

## RELATED STUDIES

One of the early contributors to social dialectology studies, Raven McDavid, Jr., grew up in a textile mill town, Greenville, South Carolina, and documented much of the social and linguistic patterning he found there (1948, 1966, 1975). The social structure of Greenville's mill villages mirrors those of Griffin (McKinley 1999) and other southeastern sites (Hall et al. 1987). McDavid reports that these insular neighborhoods were racially segregated in order to secure employment for whites without competition from African Americans. In fact, textile companies throughout the South carried over the all-white employment practice designed in 1830s South Carolina by William Gregg. This lockout of competition from lower-wage African Americans (slaves during Gregg's era) also locked out the unions. Mill workers usually lived in company villages that maintained separate churches, schools, utilities, and long-term credit stores. Mill hands came from Appalachia and unsuccessful "scratch farms" in areas that McDavid and other dialectologists traced to the Midland dialect region (versus the Southern dialect region settled earlier). By the 1940s many mill operatives were fourth-generation textile workers who stayed in the industry even though they often migrated from mill to mill in search of better wages and living conditions. At the time of his investigation, McDavid noted that tenant farming was beginning to decline; the general outlook for agriculture, especially tenant farming, is even bleaker today (Simpson and Norsworthy 1965; Wright 1986). In addition to racial segregation, McDavid (1948, 6) noted that "textile workers were originally recruited from the culturally peripheral areas, and the paternalistic company village that characterizes the Southern textile industry has created a pattern of cultural segregation as real and almost as strong as that setting off whites from Negroes." Against this backdrop, McDavid discovered that mill-worker speech usually included "lower-status" variants of the region and era, such as constricted and intrusive /r/, monophthongized /ay/, Up Country upgliding diphthongs in *date*, *boat* [deɪt, bout] (versus Low Country ingliding diphthongs [deət, boət]), and many distinctive South Midland lexical items. Although McDavid's work with the linguistic atlas project provides many insights into social and linguistic facts of the South, the task remains to carry out a sociolinguistic analysis of the relationship between social and linguistic patterns.

Crawford Feagin explores linguistic patterns using a Labovian variationist framework in her hometown of Anniston, Alabama (1990, 1994, 1997). Anniston and Griffin are similar in that they are geographically close (approximately 120 miles apart), they were both part of the early "frontier" settled by farmers moving west in the 1800s, and they both became industrialized in the early twentieth century. However, Feagin studies Anniston's speech community in terms of a hierarchical social class construct, whereas this Griffin study is focused on two separate lower economic classes. Feagin finds significant differences between upper- and working-class speech and notes that both dialects are affected by the

Southern Shift, an ongoing sound change currently under investigation by Labov and others. The Griffin study, however, does not find strong evidence that the Southern Shift is responsible for the dialect changes found in the data. In many instances, Feagin's work provides a relevant data point for comparison, and her methodology and phonetic description are referenced throughout this study.

Other investigators have explored dialect communities in which dramatic economic and linguistic changes affected local contact equations. For example, Lane (2001) investigated the birth and demise of a Danish fishing village; Cukor-Avila (1995) traced the network ties linked through a general store in rural Texas; Kerswill (2003) chronicled dialect leveling in "new" towns outside of London; and Wolfram, Hazen, and Schilling-Estes (1999) compared isolated dialects from Ocracoke and Appalachia with mainland varieties. All of these investigators found significant correlation between linguistic identity and changes in social networks and economic status that in turn affected social and linguistic patterns. Several more ongoing research programs provide relevant data points in the South, including Bailey (1997), Labov, Ash, and Boberg (1997), and Montgomery (1989).

## GRIFFIN SPEECH VARIETIES

This language contact site could be characterized in terms of a linguistically "catastrophic" event (Bailey et al. 1996). The creation of the mill villages and the attendant population influx happened very quickly. Two groups of people—white mill workers and farmers—spoke identifiably distinct dialects up through the 1940s that have become less distinct over time.[1] This linguistic setting is an excellent opportunity not only to observe language change in progress, but also to examine factors bearing on language change, such as structural markedness and social network, as well as the interaction between local ethnographic conditions and linguistic change across the South.

Based on migration patterns, regional dialectology findings, and attestations from local informants, the mill communities' founder population is traced to roots in Appalachia, while the founder

FIGURE 1.2
Griffin and Dialectology Isoglosses
(after Kurath 1949)

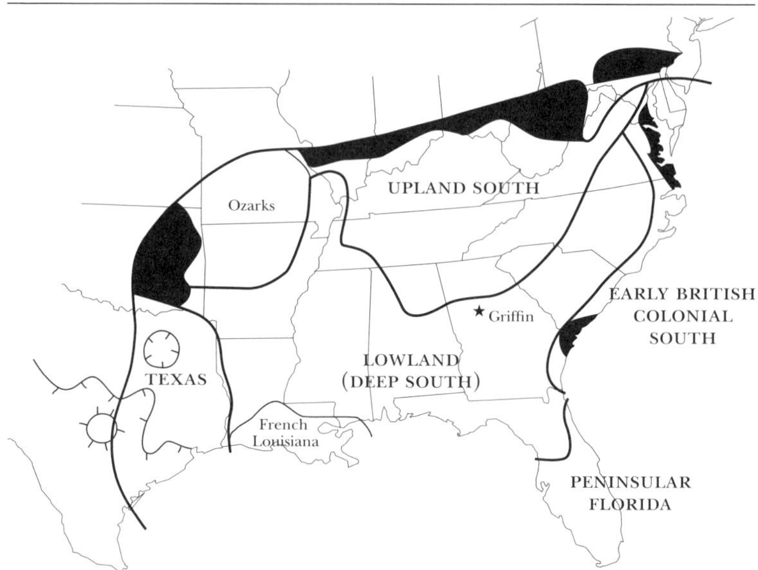


population of the farm communities were in the area earlier and probably came from the coastal areas of the southeast. Therefore, the farmers are herein correlated with Kurath's "Southern" dialect and the mill workers with Kurath's "South Midland" dialect, which also entails that these dialects stem from different geographic and linguistic sources overseas. Griffin also happens to be located near the border between the South and South Midland regions (figure 1.2). Accepting the dialectology data as valid is not an assumption that pure "transatlantic persistence" has taken place. Although the dialectologists found correlations between New World dialects and Old World dialects, it has always been apparent that changes took place throughout the passage. Repeating patterns, but not monolithic imitations, point to combination and selection of features in a process of negotiation among individual speakers. These characterizations are true for the FOUNDER POPULATIONS: the linguistic developments that may have offset the founder effect (Mufwene 1996, 1998) form the object of this study.

## FIELD METHODS

This sociolinguistic study was initiated using Milroy and Milroy's social network approach (1992; L. Milroy 1987a, 1987b) or snowball sample, which has revealed connections between individuals and led me to more and more speakers. This approach has also revealed the separateness of the two communities, suggesting that the speech community of Griffin may be a complex amalgam of groups who maintain a conflict-based evaluation of societal and linguistic norms (L. Milroy 1987a, 12–20).

The speakers in this study are "ancestral" residents, following Wolfram, Hazen, and Schilling-Estes (1999), whose families have lived in the area as either farmers or mill workers for at least three generations. Speakers were contacted through familiar network ties. In many instances, my grandmother, who grew up in a mill village but married a farmer, facilitated these meetings and sat in on the interviews. This arrangement created a casual atmosphere in which speakers talked comfortably about their past, their town, their work history, and their relationships with others. A general outline of topics was followed, but usually the interviews followed natural lines of conversation. Each informant was told that I was writing a paper on the mill and farm communities of Griffin in order to complete my doctoral degree. Interviews lasted from one to two hours and were recorded on high-quality cassette tapes using a hand-held stereo recorder and lavaliere microphones. The interviews were then transcribed into standard orthographic script, and extractions of data were scored in a separate Excel spreadsheet for each variable and each speaker. Although I conducted most of the interviews, the analytic and introspective judgments of other linguists are incorporated to produce a disciplined idealization of the data obtained through fieldwork.

SOCIAL VARIABLES. In order to focus on sites of dialect contact, this research is formulated in terms of a sample using the social variables of age, occupation, and sex (see table 1.1). Since there are few prior recordings of speech in Griffin, this study relies on the concept of apparent time to measure linguistic change. Three age groups represent three different eras significant to the social and

TABLE 1.1
Social Variables

| | *N* |
|---|---|
| Age | |
| Younger (born 1969–1982) | 12 |
| Middle Aged (born 1939–50) | 12 |
| Older (born 1898–1921) | 12 |
| Occupation | |
| Mill (mill village resident and/or worker) | 18 |
| Rural (family history in the mills) | 18 |
| Sex | |
| Female | 18 |
| Male | 18 |

economic development of Griffin. The people in the older sample were all born before 1926. They represent speakers who grew up during the Depression and became young adults during the World War II era. Bailey marks this period as a break in the parallel development of African American and white vernaculars in the South (Bailey 1993; Cukor-Avila 1995), partly as a result of the decline in farming, especially tenancy, and the concomitant migrations toward industry. This period in Griffin was also a robust environment for growth in textiles. The middle-aged group is the next generation, who grew up in the 1950s and became young adults during the 1960s. Their careers were heavily influenced by the mill economy, since farming was by then in steep decline. The younger group is composed of individuals who grew up in the 1980s. These speakers do not typically have a set career and grew up during a phase when textile mills in Griffin began to close down and farming was no longer a viable way to make a living.

Occupation is a pivotal social measurement since it encodes both regionality and social status that cannot be measured by traditional indexes of social class. Farmers and mill villagers came from different parts of the South and established residence in distinct ways. While the mill villages were dense networks with intense daily contact, farms were more spread out demographically. There was very little contact between the two groups in the older generation. Children attended different elementary schools, and many never attended high school. One older speaker characterized the social hierarchy as one of mutual disdain: "The town folks looked down on everybody, the farm kids called the mill kids lintheads, and the mill kids said the farm kids had cow [dung] between their toes." Although historically many mill workers had originally come from farms, they took pride in their work and their community, and they adopted a firm identity as villagers and skilled laborers. On the other hand, farmers adhered to a philosophy of self-sufficiency and struggled to maintain economic independence.

An equal number of men and women are presented in this sample to sufficiently account for sex as a factor in dialect identity. This linguistic contact site involves negotiation of status in an evolving economy, and these types of situations often reveal varying strategies for power used by men and women (Eckert 1989). Since occupation is one of the social variables used to determine identity in this study, every woman interviewed has a substantial work history, ensuring that occupation and social status is not a mere copy of a husband's situation (L. Milroy 1987b, 102).

LINGUISTIC VARIABLES. Dialects in the southeast have been categorized in many ways. By tracing settlement patterns and conducting extensive interviews, dialectologists identified some variants (*r*-fullness) as "South Midland" (also called Appalachian, upland, or "mountain") and others as "Southern" (*r*-lessness). However, distinctions between types of Southern dialects are not always acknowledged; in fact, most nonnative Southerners commonly conceive of only one "Southern" dialect that is relatively conservative. According to Bailey (1997), many of the linguistic variants thought of as stereotypically Southern, through public representations like films, music, and public personalities, have evolved recently, that is, within the last 100 years. For example, the merger of tense and lax vowels before /l/ in words such as *fill* and *feel* and the merger of /ɔr/ and /or/ in words such as *card* and *cord* probably formed between 1900 and 1940. Some variables have become consistent more recently, since World War II, such as glide-shortened /ay/ before voiceless obstruents in words such as *right* and *site*; and some have just begun to emerge since 1945, like the merger of /ɔ/ and /o/ in words such as *caught* and *cot*. African American varieties tend to be more conservative than white varieties (Bailey 1993, 1997); however, due to the contact equation linking African Americans and rural whites, I hypothesize that the rural variants would also be conservative.

In this volume, I will describe occurrences of both phonological and grammatical variables (table 1.2). These variables were chosen because they are relatively salient to speakers and because they are perceived as typically Southern.

TABLE 1.2
Linguistic Variables

| Old SWVE (before 1875)[a] | |
|---|---|
| Loss of /r/ constriction (independent of Southern Shift) | *work* [wɜk], *her* [hə], *four* [foə], *Virginia* [vədʒɪnyə] |
| Intrusive /r/ | *wash* [wɔrʃ] |
| Nonstandard verbs | *them girls tells me* |
| *a*-verb-*ing* | *he come a-hollerin'* |
| Perfective *done* | *she done messed up* |
| Mid SWVE (1875–1945) | |
| *pen/pin* merger (/ɛ/~/ɪ/ before nasals, independent of Southern Shift) | *pen* [pɪn] |
| *you-all/y'all* | *y'all go on home* |
| Recent SWVE (1945–1980) | |
| Merger of /ɔ/ and /o/ (independent of Southern Shift) | *caught* [kɑt] |
| Affects older feather of upgliding /ɔ/ | *caught* [kɔot] |
| Multiple modals | *she might could* |
| Quasi-modals | *fixin to, gonna* |
| The Southern Shift (chronology unclear) | |
| Back shift | *food* [fʉd]/[fʉːd], *so* [sʌʉ] |
| Front shift | *date* [da$^{i}$t], *debt* [de$^{\wedge}$t], *bit* [bi$^{\wedge}$t], *beet* [bʌ$^{i}$t] |

a. These dates of emergence are specified by Bailey (1997), who is supported by research from orthographic evidence from the Tennessee Civil War Veterans Questionnaires, the Linguistic Atlas of the Middle and South Atlantic States, Kurath and McDavid (1961), *Shorter Oxford English Dictionary*, Works Progress Administration slave narratives, Brazilian ex-Confederates, and others. Plural verbal *-s* is also classified as an older feature by Wolfram, Hazen, and Schilling-Estes (1999), who trace its origin to Scots English brought over by early settlers.

## DATA ANALYSIS

Since this study seeks to implement a multidimensional model of measuring change in dialects, the social, ethnographic, and historical factors must be accounted for. A social network model is used to assess degrees of individual integration into communities.

Social network studies consider the amount of and types of contacts individuals maintain in their community. In addition to the social variables mentioned above, network strength scales are used in this study to measure the degree of integration each individual speaker has into a close-knit group. As L. Milroy (1987b) explains, personal network structure indicates a type of social identity that may likely affect linguistic variability. An individual's social network—that is, "the sum of relationships that he or she has contracted with others" (105)—can determine how much that individual's linguistic behavior is affected by the normative pressures of close-knit groups. In Belfast, for example, Milroy found that individuals "whose personal networks were closeknit tended to approximate closely to the stigmatized vernacular norms characteristic of the locality, which like other 'in-group' norms powerfully symbolized values of solidarity, reciprocity and to some extent opposition to standardized norms along with *their* associated values" (106). Since both groups of speakers in this study are working class, a stratificational structure is an inadequate way to measure differentiating values. A better way to assess the underlying social differences is through indicators in a network strength scale that shows the extent of density and multiplexity of each speech community, individual by individual. The indicators used in this study are designed to quantify the extent to which close-knit communities in Griffin correlate to separate sets of values and separate norms. In order to determine if community is coextensive to network saturation, each speaker is assigned a network score based on five indicators to assess density and multiplexity (see table 1.3). Density correlates to Blom and Gumperz's (1972) notion of open versus closed communities; in a high-density, or closed, community, most members know each other and interact primarily within the community. These types of language communities tend to maintain low status or nonstandard dialects more than open communities

TABLE 1.3
Network Indicators

1. Residence in a high-density cluster that is centralized around one mode of economic production (marker of density).
2. Working at the same place as at least two other family members and at least the second generation of workers (marker of multiplexity).
3. Residence in same cluster as at least two family members outside nuclear family structure (marker of multiplexity).
4. Working at the same place as at least two others from the same area (marker of multiplexity).
5. Voluntary association with at least two workmates in leisure hours (marker of multiplexity).

in which members interact outside the territory with members of other communities (L. Milroy 1987a, 20). Multiplexity refers to the number of different types of contact; for instance, multiplex speakers interact in several modes, such as work, friendship, neighborhood, and kin versus a uniplex relationship that depends solely on one type of interaction. When members of a community work, live, and marry together, the norm enforcement role of the community is usually quite strong. Following Milroy's network study of three clusters in the Belfast area (1987a, 141–42), measurements of social network in this study are gauged by assigning one point for each of the following five indicators a speaker fulfills. As in Milroy's framework, the first condition is an indicator of density, while the other four indicate multiplexity. Because many of the speakers are elderly, the conditions assigned to them were those that were fulfilled during the period of time when they were working.

## SUMMARY

The emphasis of this investigation is to determine how the language contact equation between two speech communities in Griffin has played out over the past century of dramatic economic cycles. Acknowledging that language is an object that can reflect abstract structures difficult to observe directly, a multidimensional approach is implemented to present the data informed by linguistic, anthropological, sociological, and statistical methods.

# 2. SETTLEMENT PATTERNS, CULTURAL SPACE, AND LINGUISTIC EVOLUTION IN THE AMERICAN SOUTH

Language evolution can be productively analogized to a model of combination and selection of features, as in Mufwene (2000b), which are in part formed by and often in turn create patterns of identity and group membership that defy simple concepts of race, class, or regionality. The South is a region that has been imagined and reimagined in geographic, linguistic, racial, and cultural terms. In this equation of individuals within a simultaneously concrete and abstract entity, some structures carry over while other factors change. Taking these exigencies into account, speech communities within this region can be specified ethnographically as imaginary geographies demarcated not by official boundaries but by perceptible political, economic, and cultural lines (Said 1979). Divisions between mill villagers and farmers in the South are instantiations not only of occupational difference but also of complex identity constructs that rely on intraregionality, family and network ties, and class.

Writers about the South have identified two ways of assessing the history and identity of the region: some mark a significant break occurring with the end of the Civil War and Reconstruction, while others assert that the current cultural patterns of the South can be closely compared to the past and even identified as "reproductions of history" (Hahn 1983). Furthermore, investigators have struggled to validate a definition of the South as a separate, concrete region, and many have resorted to evocations of the region in psychological terms of "the idea of the South," the South as "written," and the South as mistakenly regionalized in terms of contrast and conflict with the "normal" rest of the United States. Such marginalization of the South was compounded by Roosevelt's depiction of it as the "number one economic problem" of the nation during the 1930s, which deepened an "identity crisis" that had taken root after the Civil War (Van Hoosier-Carey 1999). The present study works on a smaller, even more local level of regionality and identity and thereby assumes at the very least that a bit of the national imagination of the South presupposes and thus allows further specification on the validity of the trait "Southern." The local level of the mill village within the agricultural terrain of middle Georgia presents bounded spaces formed within intersecting lines of history, economics, intraregionality, and dialect. Examining a specific case within a larger, known context sheds light on existent speculations; and previous work on both the regionality and sectionalism of the South serves as a guide both to recorded and unrecorded history.

Linguistically, the South has always been remarked upon for both its distinctiveness within the United States and for the diversity within the region itself. While much of this diversity has been aptly described, this study explores the selection processes that have resulted in not only persistent variation, but also consistent underlying social meaning. Coexistent with dissimilarities is a plethora of similarities; in fact, the trajectory of speech varieties may be analogical to the evolution of pidgins, creoles, and other English varieties in the New World.

## LOCAL SPEECH COMMUNITIES

Founded in the 1840s, Griffin's socioeconomic history is one of passive-aggressive entrepreneurialism. Griffin's local speech communities are not old and not permanent. Group formations have been susceptible to dramatic shifts caused by the unstable economies of farming and industry. Founded as a farming community with high hopes of cotton commerce as a major railroad intersection, Griffin has always seemed to "have potential." Mill builders certainly thought so in the late 1800s—post–Civil War during the Reconstruction Era—when they set up an economy for a whole new population; and farmers thought so far past the years of the boll weevil, the Depression, and the disfranchisement of small operators. However, at the end of the twentieth century, it seems evident that the sun has set on both the textile and the farm economic engines: open lands rapidly disappear as the area is paved for ex-urbanites, and closed mills loom in the middle of ghost-ridden mill villages. The remains of yesterday's communities can only be found in the persistent cultural identity of the residents who remember a time when they belonged somewhere. Their shared psychological experience of "belonging" was quite strong when Griffin was polarized according to occupation, which also physically divided communities by urban and rural terrains.

FARMERS. No matter how one assesses the history and identity of the region, it remains a fact that the Civil War left agricultural regions in the interior South in a state of disarray. Faced with the absence of slave labor, many farm owners either sold off land or rented portions of their land to farm tenants. Although the tenancy system was economically unprofitable for the white and African American tenant farmers, it did grant both whites and African Americans some semblance of independence and self-sufficiency. Tenancy expanded until 1930, then dwindled to near extinction by 1970 (see table 2.1, taken from Gavin Wright's discussion on the decline of tenancy in the South [1986, 226–49]). This decline was due largely to measures of Roosevelt's New Deal, which gave farm

TABLE 2.1
Declining Number of Farm Operators in the South
(adapted from Wright 1986, 245)

| | *White* | | *African American* | |
|---|---|---|---|---|
| *Year* | *Owners* | *Tenants* | *Owners* | *Tenants* |
| 1930 | 1,250 | 1,092 | 183 | 699 |
| 1940 | 1,384 | 943 | 173 | 507 |
| 1945 | 1,526 | 690 | 189 | 476 |
| 1950 | 1,553 | 540 | 193 | 366 |
| 1954 | 1,454 | 399 | 181 | 283 |
| 1959 | 1,151 | 228 | 128 | 138 |
| 1964 | 1,017 | 171 | 102 | 82 |
| 1969 | 953 | 118 | 72 | 18 |

owners indirect financial incentive to employ more wage earners rather than provide land for tenant farmers.[1] This trend increased mobility among farm workers, especially the African Americans, who started to move in search of better jobs. Although much of this migration was directed out of the South to the North, there were also significant movements within the South to various industrial centers.

Before this point, most farmers were long-time residents of the area they worked in. Many of the farmers I interviewed were landowners, but they did not start off with land of their own. A common scenario was dependence upon family until one could buy one's own land. One extended family housed eight people in a four-room house, including three married couples. People who could not buy their own land were at the mercy of the injustices of the tenant system, a product of both entrenched landowner hierarchy and workings of the federal assistance programs.

MILL WORKERS. There were two major periods of migration to the mill towns in the South. The first occurred during the 1890s and early 1900s, when the original mills were built. Many mill villagers trace their origins to other mill towns, and before that to the hills of Alabama or north Georgia (McDavid 1966; Hall et al. 1987; McKinley 1999). For example, one mill worker's grandfather came from another mill town, Phenix City, Alabama, in 1908 and sharpened drill bits for the crew that dynamited the local granite; then he helped lay the granite foundation for the bleachery; and finally he was signed on as a mill hand. His family has been employed in the mill ever since. In fact, by the 1950s, the mills in Griffin were largely staffed by third- and even fourth-generation workers. The second wave of migration came in the 1940s, after World War II. Many men just coming home from war, both single and with families, shifted around from mill to mill until they found steady jobs. Women also worked in the mills, often during their teenage years. During the period immediately following the war, the mills offered jobs to a large portion of the sudden influx of unemployed men. Almost all of the people whom I asked, "Did you like working at the mill?" replied that it wasn't a matter of liking, you just took what you could get.

TABLE 2.2
Decreased Number of Farms and Increased Manufacturing in Spalding County, 1890–1950
(adapted from U.S. Historical Census Data Browser)

| *Year* | *No. of Farms* | *No. of Manufacturers* | *No. of Mfg. Wage Earners* | *No. of Males of Voting Age* |
|---|---|---|---|---|
| 1890 | 922 | 55 | 667 | 1,033 |
| 1900 | 1,272 | 49 | 1,039 | 1,619 |
| 1910 | 1,727 | no data | no data | 2,455 |
| 1920 | 1,882 | 33 | 2,112 | 4,257 |
| 1930 | 1,128 | 34 | 3,538 | 3,925 |
| 1940 | 850 | 38 | 5,224 | 7,786 |
| 1950 | 833 | no data | no data | 7,760 |

Once established in mill jobs, villagers resisted changes that threatened their relatively isolated communities. Roy (1965) describes the early mill owner as the "Uncle Ben" of a "benevolent paternalism" in the feudalistic structure of the mill community. The workers' affection for the owner checked any aggressive movements for advancement. For instance, Roy relates a story of Georgia mill workers who did not "vote in" a union until the former owner of the mill died, because "it would break his heart if he heard that they joined a union" (239). Mill workers in this study claim that they were opposed to unions because the mills provided cheap housing and the best wages in town. Indeed, the mills not only survived but even prospered at full-time operation in the midst of the Depression (McKinley 1999, 2). The most vivid memory of unionization is of the Highland Mill closing in 1934. The event was so volatile that reportedly 250 national guardsmen were called in to keep the peace (Melton 1996). Furthermore, "Many of the workers and activists ended up in court, as friendships were threatened and jobs lost. Some workers were threatened that they might be denied the right ever to work in textiles again because of their involvement with union leaders" (McKinley 1999, 4). Other historians explain Southern resistance to unions by citing mill owners' threats to hire African Americans instead of union members, playing on the fear and resentment built up between African Americans and poor whites (Caldwell and Bourke-White 1937). In contrasting the "village" in Europe and the United States, McDavid (1975) emphasizes the effects of uniformity and diversity in the U.S. system on cultural identity, including language. To this end, he even suggests the existence of mill villagers as a "third race" in the American South. Declaring a group of people as a separate race in the South is perhaps about as strong a statement as one could make, especially in the sensitive pre–Civil Rights era that McDavid described. Not only did McDavid study Greenville, South Carolina, a textile mill town, but he also grew up in it. His impressions of mill villagers as culturally and almost ethnically separate reveal the compounded nature of their separation from the other communities in the region: town people, African Americans, and farmers.

AFRICAN AMERICANS. In rural areas, African Americans were often tenant farmers or sharecroppers on the same farms that their enslaved ancestors worked during the plantation era. Wright (1986, 88, 92) illustrates typical spatial reorganization of plantations after the Civil War in which former slave quarters were broken up into houses scattered over individual plots of land (figure 2.1). In this scenario, African Americans very likely maintained some contact with the white farm owners and tenant farmers. However, these social network ties, once quite dense, faded with the decline of farm tenancy that plummeted from 1945 to 1969. In other words, the decrease of farm tenancy led to the decline of the social fabric of the community's previous identity.

Unlike the steel mills in Alabama, textile mills in Georgia did not include African Americans in the workforce, probably because African Americans had a history of skills in steelworking, but not in textiles (Simpson and Norsworthy 1965, 207). The only exceptions in the mills of Griffin were a cleaning lady and a maintenance man, and whites sometimes filled even these positions. Other common occupations for African Americans included working at the local laundry, filling household positions such as cooks, maids, and nannies, and working manual labor jobs. Once the African American population was integrated into the mill workforce, it was only to fill the lower positions left vacant by whites: Southern industry's "whites, still in control of its economy, have reaped most of the

FIGURE 2.1
Tenant Farm Patterns after the Civil War
(Woofter 1936, xxxii; reproduced in Wright 1986, 92)

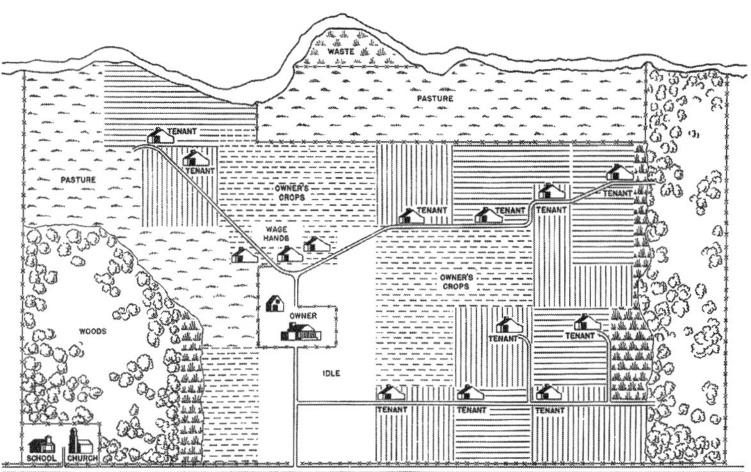


NOTE: This figure is a composite based on 646 typical cotton plantations.

fruits of its progress; southern Negroes are in some ways more disadvantaged than ever in the region's occupational structure" (222–23). The African American community, therefore, cannot be neatly delineated by occupation. Although the white community at large was also more diverse than the sample described herein, the cohesive communities of mill workers and farmers remained intact and describable for quite some time, at least until the integration of the mills in the early 1970s, and arguably up to the first major mill closings in the early 1980s.

Nevertheless, it is certain that African Americans played a significant early role in the linguistic contact equation. Although tracing the modern trajectory of African American Vernacular English (AAVE) is beyond the scope of this study, examining the historical influence of African American varieties on the development of white varieties (if only by self-differentiation) is essential, especially on contact sites in settlement history.

## SETTLEMENT PATTERNS

By tracing patterns of migration and settlement, many scholars have argued that settlers in the New World followed consistent outlines already established in the Old World. Individuals in specific demographies left the same parts of England at the same time and arrived in the same places in the New World. In this general reproduction of previous cultural groupings, many factors tended to be reproduced in the new setting, but the complete contact equation in each new setting was unique.

PATHS OF MIGRATION. The earliest wave of migrants to the South has been described as a "metropolitan pattern," consisting of single, male indentured servants and well-off Englishmen from London and the Thames Valley to the mid-Atlantic colonies before the revolution (Bailyn 1988) (see fig. 2.2). This odd mix of enterprising "distressed cavaliers" and indentured servants (about 75% of the population) left the south and west of England between 1642 and 1675 (Fischer 1989, 215). After the peace treaty of 1763, a larger, second wave of nonindentured families came from territories that bordered the Irish Sea (fig. 2.3) (Bailyn 1988, 75). There were also many Germans, and Georgia was probably "polyglot" (Bailyn 1988, 16–17). Towns were established in the frontier regions, with the farthest western Georgia counties established in the early to mid-1800s (Hahn 1983; Bailyn 1988).

The "folkways" described by Fischer (1989, 275) loosely delineate two characterizations between the first and second waves of migrants to the South. While the earlier settlers were associated with wealthy established families who stayed in England, the Scotch-Irish fled with their families from war, famine and poverty. Furthermore, the first wave of travelers tended to increase their wealth in the new world and extended their reach by both buying land and intermarrying in "cousinages" and establishing "kin-neighborhoods." The land they acquired was located first in the Chesapeake colonies, then along the coasts and in the southern interior region where soil was nutrient-rich and could support lucrative crops. By the time the second wave arrived from the margins of northern England, Ireland, and Scotland, there was little

FIGURE 2.2
Origins of First Wave Migrants to the South
(after Fischer 1989, 238)

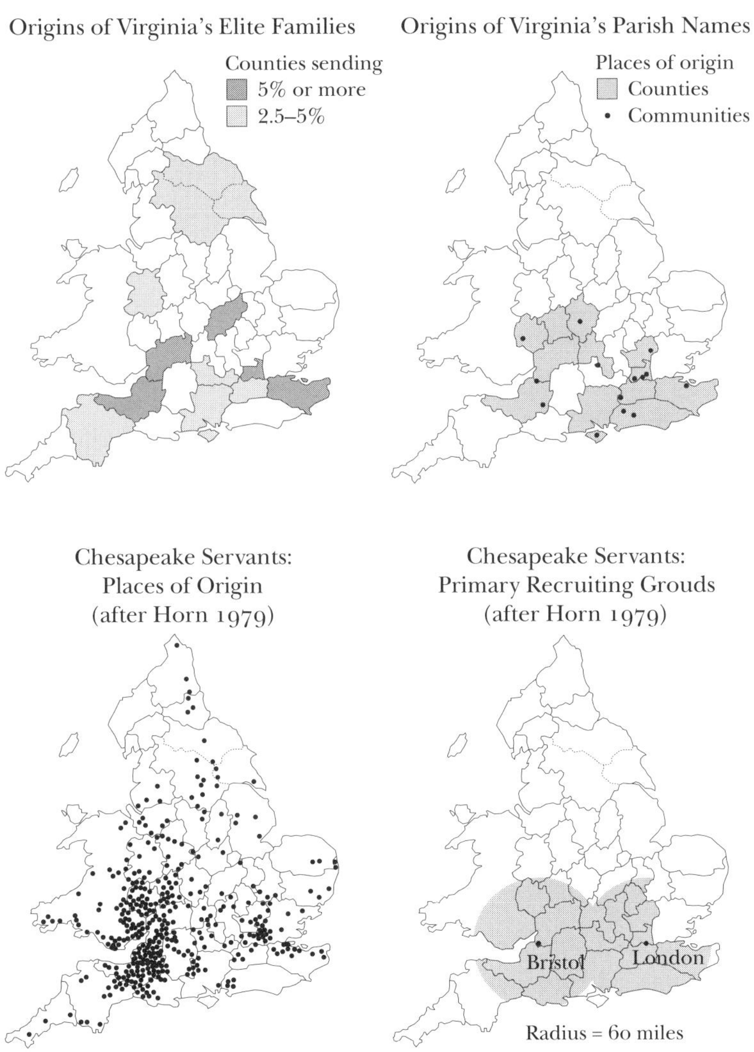

FIGURE 2.3
Origins of Later Migrants to the South
(after Fischer 1989, 607)

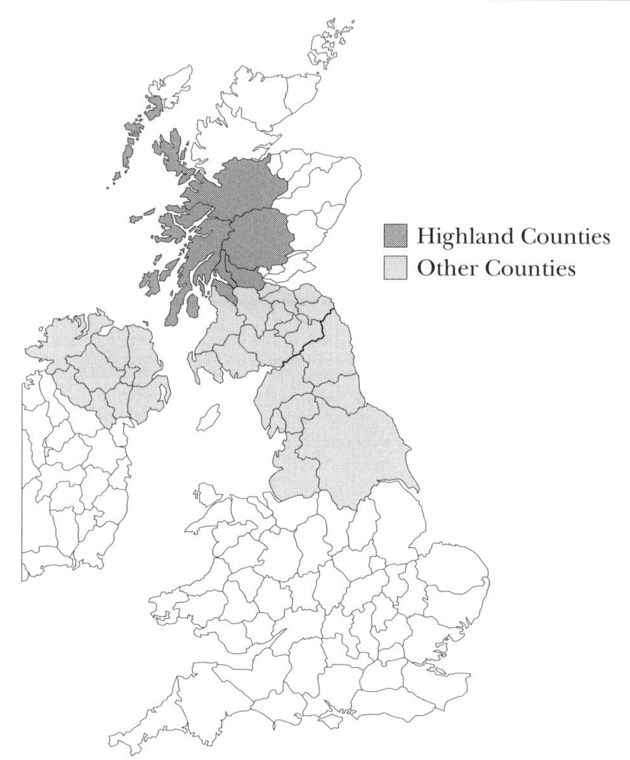


work in the overcrowded cities, and much of the land was taken by the earlier migrants and their extended families. Residual prejudice helped shunt these already tight-knit, clan-based families into the frontier regions of the Piedmont and along the southern spine of the isolated Appalachians. This pattern of settlement was little more than a continuation of separations that had existed in the homeland. They arrived with variations of dialects and cultural ways that had been distinct for generations prior.

THE DETERMINISTIC ROLE OF GEOGRAPHY (AND ECONOMICS). Georgia is typically described as consisting of two regions: (1) the coastal and Deep South areas, which early on were used for rice, indigo, and cotton plantations, and (2) the Piedmont and northern regions, which were settled later and supported small-scale farming. There is also a part of northern Georgia where the tail end of the Appalachians runs in a swath from the North Carolina border all the way into northern Alabama. That terrain is mountainous and rocky, supportive of only minimal farming.

The physical geography was the foundation of cultural geographies constructed by intersections of crop success and human capital. Many early Georgians arrived via the first wave in the Chesapeake colonies as indentured servants from parts of western Europe. These servants earned their freedom and became farmers alongside former masters, sometimes even intermarrying into those families (Cash 1941). However, indentured servitude was soon replaced by African workers obtained through the slave trade, an institution that would make the large plantation economy possible and therefore shape the South as a region with indelible class distinctions based not only on skin color, but also on land ownership (Cash 1935; Hahn 1983). The largest plantations were established on the southern Atlantic coast along the barrier islands. These rice and indigo plantations required hundreds of slaves, were often owned by absentee landlords and managed by white overseers, and resulted in some of the most appalling living conditions for slaves anywhere in the United States (Kemble 1961; Mufwene 1997). Although the interior regions never approximated this large-scale plantation economy, early settlers in the Piedmont were likely descendants of the first blacks and whites who worked side by side as indentured servants (Mufwene 2000b). Records from Griffin show that early citizens came from coastal communities in the southeast, often from Savannah, South Carolina, and North Carolina (Melton 1996).

The interior regions of the state, considered the "frontier" up through the mid-1800s, offered poorer farming conditions, but still provided sustenance for a brief reign of a yeoman class (1840–90, according to Hahn 1983). Eventually, the whole Piedmont fell under the sway of King Cotton. Cotton was the cash crop, and it became an obsession with farmers that lasted long after the soil was depleted. By the time of the Great Depression in the 1930s, the most money made from cotton land was reaped by landowners who, having already exhausted the soil's potential, exploited sharecroppers and tenant farmers still trying to wrench a living from ruined land (witness Caldwell and Bourke-White 1937 and Agee and Evans 1941).

Griffin was largely settled by an ambitious planter class who sought to establish a cotton mecca by placing themselves at the intersection of an east-west and north-south railroad in the middle of the farming Piedmont (see fig. 2.4). General Lawrence Lewis Griffin explicitly planned the town around a potential railroad crossing that would locate Griffin at the center of heavy commerce and transportation in the Southeast. However, like many such projects across the Georgia landscape, his endeavor went bankrupt before the east-west line could be built, and the business center he planned materialized for others in the town of Atlanta (née Terminus, then Marthasville). So, before the Civil War, Griffin was a struggling trading town that shipped in, processed, and stored cotton from the surrounding farmland. A traveler of the time described the terrain:

> I look out on a rough sort of flat, scattered over which one might count, perhaps, sixty or seventy houses; stumps, of course, everywhere except on the railway that terminates opposite. At a little distance I read on a small one-storey house, 'Broadway Exchange.' Bags of cotton lie profusely scattered about the railway. A picture of one among many of these ... populous towns pushed by these pushing people into existence and name. Around is the everlasting wood. Some signs are on cloth, instead of board. Trees and stumps alternate through the city, and cotton, cotton everywhere. [Macready 1912; quoted in Melton 1996, 23]

As soon as travelers leave on the "plank road" that stood in for the bankrupt rail line, they are immediately in the pastoral scenery of rural Georgia: "The country was wood, beautiful in its various fields of cotton and corn, stalks continually appearing in the newly cleared woods" (23). Griffin's population included townspeople, such as lawyers, dentists, and storekeepers, but most of the people who settled the region were "cotton men." For a while, Griffin even

FIGURE 2.4
Map of Georgia Counties and Railroads, circa 1879
(after Cram 1879)

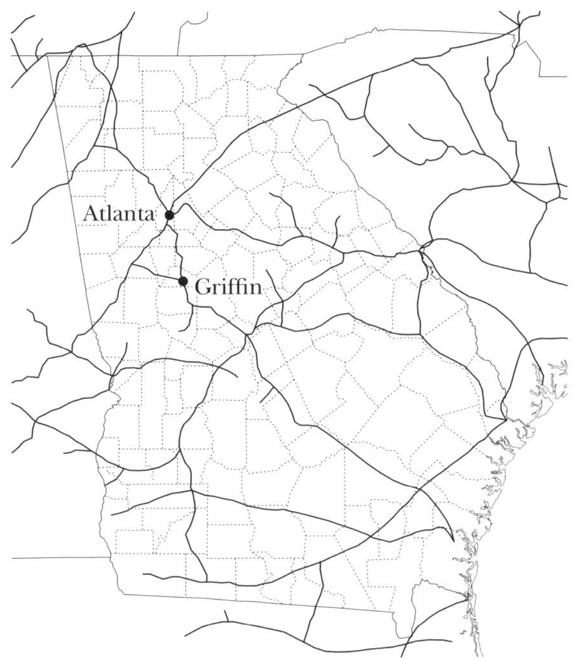


had a slave-trading company. However, it is not clear how profitable this business was, for the deed records of Griffin before the Civil War record very low numbers of slave ownership (the richest men had eight to ten slaves), and many of the slaves were domestic servants and their children (Purdy 1983; Melton 1996).

In the Upcountry and the Appalachians to the north was a rather different breed of settler. First of all, the terrain, soil, and climate became hillier, rockier, and cooler further northward. These farmers had land rich enough to feed their families, but the soil could not support enough product for a sufficient cash crop, though some managed to bring in small cotton crops to trade for goods (Hahn 1983, 45). These more conservative people distrusted the market, so they avoided growing purely for cash, anyway.

It became apparent as early as the 1860s that few small farmers owned enough good land to become large planters; they instead diversified and began to grow more food crops. Although land values rose, the lack of profit made it impossible for most families to increase their holdings among numerous heirs, who were needed to work the land in the first place (48–49). Farmers of the mountainous regions were often unable to continue supporting their families, and positions in industry, when introduced in Georgia in the 1880s, were an appealing alternative for many. However, such a move usually meant giving up one's land and home or leaving one's family. Many families chose to pack up and move everything to the mill villages.

Griffin's history is strikingly similar to that of Greenville, South Carolina, where Raven I. McDavid, Jr., grew up and later did research. Greenville was probably first settled by a group of farmers, a small elite, and house servants of African descent. The African American population never dominated demographically, and many became tenant farmers after emancipation. The racially segregated cotton mills introduced in the late nineteenth century "were staffed by displaced or unsuccessful farmers from the mountains and other unproductive areas, though by now textile employment has become a hereditary way of life for the fourth generation" (McDavid 1966, 37). This pattern was likely replicated throughout the South.

MIGRATIONS AND CULTURAL SPACES. While a minority planter class did initiate and engineer much of Griffin's early plans, the general early and later populations would consist of a diverse lower class. Griffin was a borderline community situated between two subregions, the Upcountry and the Plantation Belt (see figure 2.5), that became a locus of contact and conflict. At the time when Griffin was founded in the early 1840s, three distinct cultural spaces were emerging. The established, wealthy planter class resided in the mid-to-southern part of the state in the Plantation Belt, or Black Belt. Backcountry residents were still holding their ground in the north Georgia mountains, and a growing population of small-scale farmers, or yeomen, who were often related to the wealthy planters, settled most of the Upper Piedmont, termed the "Upcountry."

FIGURE 2.5
Georgia Regions, circa 1880
(after Hahn 1983, 7)

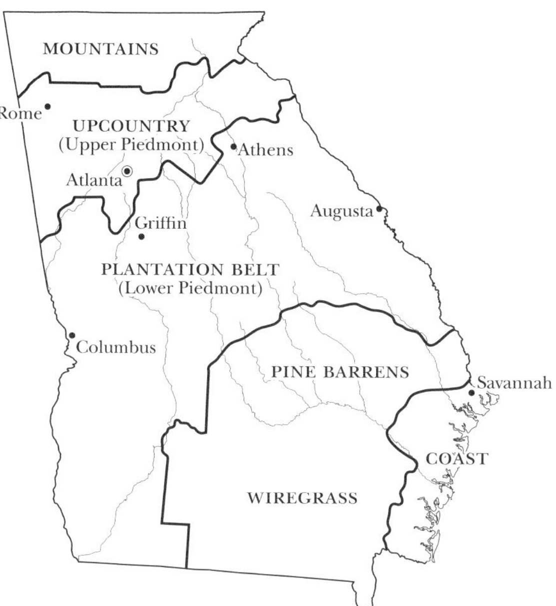


The backcountry farmers were effectively separated from the other groups both geographically and culturally, and these patterns were probably not accidental. For example, most of the indentured servants who came with the first wave, with the planter class, were from south and southwest England because "Virginia's great migration was the product of policy and social planning. Its royalist elite succeeded in shaping the social history of an American region partly by regulating the process of migration" (Fischer 1989, 232). These early indentured servants worked out their time and became freedmen and landowners. Several accounts posit that these freedmen and the planter class they formerly worked for maintained intimate ties in the forms of interdependent farming and trade, neighborhoods, and even kin (Cash 1941; Hahn 1983). On the other hand, when the borderlands families entered these regions, they were reviled as undesirables and forcefully encouraged to keep moving on. They ended up as "buffers" to the frontier in the backcountry, thus reenacting the geographic isolation many of them lived out in the British Isles.

The Upcountry farmers were not quite as isolated as the residents of Appalachia and engaged in frequent commerce with planters in the Plantation Belt (Hahn 1983, 51). In fact, many Upcountry and Plantation Belt farmers of this yeoman class were products of earlier cotton plantations. Contrasted with the borderlands migrants to the north, these farmers were part of the earlier migrations that included both wealthy and poor classes. However, the large cotton-plantation owners, the slaveholders, were more deeply entrenched, wealthier men who were heavily invested in the causes of the Civil War. The people in the Upcountry worked small farms of diversified agriculture with very few slaves. Although cotton was king enough to link the South to the rest of the world economically, these farmers were distrustful of the market and preferred to work and live within cooperative communities. They also may have recognized that the one-crop system was still little more advanced than a home-grown feudalistic system. For a brief period, economic interests twinned with ethical and political interests, and the populist movement (the topic of Hahn's study) took hold in some regions of north Georgia. Although the Upcountry farmers tried to live in noncapitalistic, semisubsistence communities, their region underwent a forced shift to commercial agriculture between 1860 and 1900 (9).

On a local level, class conflict between planters and the yeomanry of the Upcountry in Georgia existed as early as the 1840s (Hahn 1983). Issues of slaveholding, land ownership, and autonomy in resistance to market interests divided these groups long before the Civil War. Hahn differentiates between farmers in the two regions: "Black Belt yeomen lived in a society dominated by planters and plantations; Upcountry yeomen in a society dominated by farmers and farms. If they shared a broadly similar economic status, they resided in very different worlds" (27). Pro-Unionist and antislavery factions in Georgia came mainly from Upcountry counties, but planters attempted to control even that political and agricultural landscape. The Civil War itself exacerbated this schism since, ironically, many of the soldiers and many of the battles were based in the Upcountry. The poorer classes were "impressed" to give up their fathers, husbands, and sons to the Confederacy, to give up their livestock and crops to soldiers, and to give up their surplus to a "tax-in-kind" in support of the war effort. The resentment that resulted is summed up by a Floyd county farmer:

> Is it right that the poor man should be taxed for the support of the war, when the war was brought about on the slave question, and the slave at home accumulating for the benefit of his master, and the poor man's farm left uncultivated, a chance for his wife to be a widow, and his children orphans? Now, in justice, would it not be right to levy a direct tax on that species of property that brought about the war to support it? [Hahn 1983, 26]

In addition to these impingements, Confederate soldiers resorted to pillaging and looting farms of Upcountry farmers in the name of legal impressments (127). Soon, Sherman's soldiers would follow suit, and the culmination of the Civil War for the poor was further impoverishment, leading to the kind of resentment that festered through Reconstruction and beyond.

Of course there is no absolute geographic line between the Upcountry and the Plantation Belt. For a while, people from both areas navigated "complex ties of kinship and quasi-dependen[ce]," but this became increasingly difficult due to "methods of land cultivation and accumulation that served at once to exhaust soil and strain class relations" (16). Although many of these economically disparate people were intimately related through social ties, business, and kin, foundational tensions led to patterns of "increasing concentration of wealth and power [and] new conditions of dependency" (Hahn 1983, 2). After the Civil War, economic disparities plagued the just-conquered frontier of northern and western Georgia and resulted in struggles between small farmers insulated from cash economy and cotton cash crop farmers creating intake to a capitalist industry. At the end of the nineteenth century, these tensions were intensified by the influx of mill workers into the exploitative textile mill industry. With local resources nearby, plenty of cheap land, and desperate labor spilling in from failed farms, this area offered a comfortable seat for textile entrepreneurs to sit just atop Deep South cotton country.

IMAGINARY GEOGRAPHIES. In this setting, the mills established factories and villages that attracted first the poorest farmers, that is, those from the isolated, poor lands of Appalachia. A "spindleage map" generated by Hall et al. (1987) from 1929 and 1930 figures reflects the parallel development of geographical and cultural areas in the southward spread of textiles (fig. 2.6). Even within Spalding County, and within the city limits of Griffin, the social status of these descendants of borderlands migrants relegated them to isolation in the social fringe. Mill villagers, often having lost farms or reached economic incapacity, had opted to become part of the feudalistic mill system where everything was provided by an employer. These people were looked down on, even though the mill workers were sometimes earning a better living. In Carson McCullers's (1940) saga of a Georgia mill town, *The Heart Is a Lonely Hunter*, Mick says of her bankrupt family, "They were mighty near as poor

FIGURE 2.6
Spindleage Map of the Southeast, circa 1930
(Hall et al. 1987, map 1)

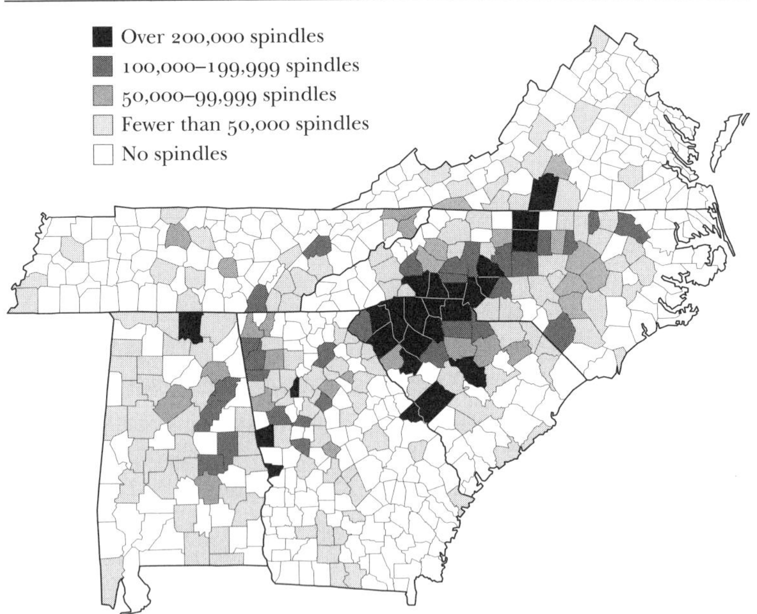

as factory folks. Only nobody could look down on them" (203). This attitude in part stems from the commonplace distrust of the market and the sensed connection between land ownership and self-sufficiency. "Associat[ing] freedom and independence with landownership" may have been a national trope, says Hahn (1983, 50). But in the South, "slavery itself strengthened claims to this cultural baggage, not only by serving as a stark reminder of the consequences of dependency, but also by limiting the development of directly exploitative, market relations between whites."

The mill villagers had never modeled themselves on the rich planter's life, while many small-scale farmers did—both ideologically and monetarily. The disconnect between the ideology and the fiscal reality impaired both the individual's ability to progress financially as well as the region's ability to recover from the social and physical damage of the Civil War. Cash emphasizes the blood-and-money link between upper and lower classes in his anthropomorphizing depiction, *The Mind of the South* (1941). This part of the Southern psyche, this fantastic nostalgia, was a major binding factor in communities throughout the "problem South" where worth was rigidly determined by rites and rights of membership. Likewise, the social boundary that separated mill workers from farmers resulted in tight-knit groups of allegiance. The fact that the mill villages were first stocked with the very poor, combined with established patterns of isolation and lingering prejudices founded decades before, encouraged a class distinction based primarily on attitude rather than pure economic status. But the mill villagers also engendered group status that is not only typified as "family," but also as class. Mill villager Judy McKinley dedicates her book to her fellow workers and neighbors:

> A worthy class of people whose only pride came from what they learned, and yes, even loved: their jobs, their experiences, and the knowledge gained, not from books, but from actual, hands-on work and from each other. Their values were real. [1999, 11]

"Real values" translates into dense networks of not only work and neighborhood, but also school, church, recreation, and commerce. McKinley notes that "the tendency to marry neighbors and co-workers played a major role in giving the 'mill family' cohesiveness" (47). In addition to this occupational endogamy, the idea of community entailed boundaries and membership requirements of individuals eager to join a social order. For example, one mill villager related her childhood as a very lonely existence. She grew up in a mill village in Griffin, characterized repeatedly as "just like a family" by fellow villagers. However, she was not allowed to attend the village elementary school because her mother had been blackballed for participating in a mill strike. As she and her family learned, "The Mill was not just a job." Likewise, marrying across community lines was uncommon. In one farm family, gatherings grew sparse and tense when the matriarch refused to condone her son's marriage to a mill-born girl.

Today, the political terrain that was always marked by the prestige dialect of the planter class has begun to shift. John Edwards, the Democratic vice presidential candidate in 2004, called on his mill village roots and identified with the working class and a nationwide pattern of disfranchisement:

> And today, I see their faces. I see the faces of the men and women who worked in the mill in Robbins, North Carolina—the mill my father worked in, the mill I worked in. I can picture their faces as clear as they are in front of me right now, lint in their hair and grease on their faces, men and women who represent the best of what America is.
>
> They went to work day after day, decade after decade in the mill because they believed that if they worked hard and did what was right, they could build a better life for themselves and their families. [John Edwards Home Page, http://www.johnedwards2004.com/home.asp (accessed June 7, 2004)]

However, in 1938, President Roosevelt, backed by extensive sociological research by Howard W. Odum of the University of North Carolina, declared that the South was the nation's "Number One Economic Problem."[2] In the South, this announcement incited public debates that were probably flare-ups from earlier contentious views that either the South should be left alone, implying that Reconstruction had wreaked havoc and caused the depressive economy, versus voices against the ongoing system that encouraged poverty and race conflicts that had only worsened in the twentieth century. Woodward (1974, 69) argues, for instance, "The South's adoption of extreme racism was due not so much to a conversion as it was to a relaxation of the opposition. All the elements of fear, jealousy, proscription, hatred, and fanaticism had long been present." The complex mix of different southern views further belies the image of the South as a unified, monolithic culture. However, within and unto itself, the South can also be seen as carrying over problems that resulted from repetitive patterns. W. J. Cash (1938) pointed this out in the *Charlotte News*:

> Rather, it is the inevitable outcome of a vast complex of historical forces. One of those is slavery and what has come down to us from slavery—a social system in which economic ends are continually secured by considerations of racial feeling—a surplus of labor cheaper than that to be had anywhere else in America—the competition of the Negro with the white man, and the consequent beating down of the living standard of the latter—and the army of cheap Negro labor living in slums, dealt out a most inadequate justice in our courts, and left to wallow in poverty, crime, and disease, with inevitable results on the social status, the crime-rate and health of the white race—and so on and so on.

This view appears in myriad sources both sociological and literary. In *The Heart Is a Lonely Hunter*, McCullers's socially concerned characters argue against each other for the rights of poor whites versus African Americans, and each case sounds tragically alike. Specifically, the local mill village inspires outrage:

> 'Back to our mill village,' Jake said. 'A young linthead begins working at the fine wage of eight or ten dollars a week at such times as he can get himself employed. He marries. After the first child the woman must work in the mill also. Their combined wages come to say eighteen dollars a week when they both got work. Huh! They pay a fourth of this for the shack the mill provides them. They buy food and clothes at a company-owned or dominated store. The store overcharges on every item. With three or four younguns they are held down the same as if they had on chains. That is the whole principle of serfdom. Yet here in America we call ourselves free. And the funny thing is that this has been drilled into the heads of sharecroppers and lintheads and the rest so hard that they really believe it. But it's taken a hell of a lot of lies to keep them from knowing.' [1940, 256]

Wright (1986) notes that the mill village system was constructed to attract and retain workers from backcountry areas. The development of the industry, additionally, was dependent upon "the adaptation by these people, not just to the factory and the tasks, but to the entire social setting, to industrial employment as a life's work and a way of life" (125). Odum (1936, 135) notes, "A third group approximating a social class is the mill village worker, who has emerged through the new and distinctive decentralized industry which has followed some of the patterns of the Old South in the control and dominance of its workers," that is, a "plantation-like"—or coal mine–like—feudalism. Describing an environment of mutual distrust, McDavid (1966, 38) took the division a step further: "So strong were the economic and social barriers setting off the mill district from the town that it used to be said, not altogether in jest, that Greenville [S.C.] was a community of three races—whites, Negroes and cotton-mill workers."

Yet, the mill villagers themselves record the scene from a different perspective. Hall et al.'s investigation, *Like a Family: The Making of a Southern Cotton Mill World* (1987), chronicles the conflicted affection that mill workers felt for early paternalistic mill owners and continued to feel for their invented community. McKinley's (1999) homemade interviews and commentary painfully trace the deep sense of loss most villagers felt when the mills began to close down. The factory workers in the Federal Writers' Project's *These Are Our Lives* (1939) speak well of the owners and managers; in fact, the editor doubts "whether any owners have ever spoken better for themselves" (xii). In the same preface, the general assessment of the contributors is that "the farm laborer and his family in the South are near the bottom of the social pyramid. Beneath them in economic and social status are only such groups as the down and out and almost hopeless unemployed not on relief, the derelicts, tramps, bums and criminals" (xiv). In his 1936 survey, Odum found, "in terms of an adequate farming economy," that "the Southeast, in comparison with the mode of other regions, lags in every item of a twelve-point scale" (47). Indeed, the social hierarchy of the twentieth-century South seemed to preclude the existence of a middle class.[3] Especially during the period between the two world wars, a pathos of fear and desperation gripped the many-varied lower classes. In the mills, any job was a step up, and jobs were jealously guarded. This attitude prevented successful unionization, barricaded communities so that exclusion was the rule, and solidified cultural identity that persisted from other eras. Farmers struggled with the boll weevil, the National Recovery Administration, the economic strictures of cotton, and the lasting damage already done to the soil. Despite periods of crisis and "catastrophic" shifts, certain continuities endured. The distinctions within the Southern lower classes are intricate constructs of history, economics, heritage, and group membership.

## LINGUISTIC PATTERNS

By the time the cultural spaces of Griffin were thoroughly entrenched, several migrations had taken place. While the majority of original mill villagers came from Appalachia and upper Piedmont regions, their dialect must have already undergone much accommodation. In fact, according to Mufwene (2000a), the nature of most New World dialects was dependent upon speakers of different varieties acquiring different target varieties. In an appropriately complex assessment of socioeconomic history, the influence of both metapopulations and founder populations is significant. The term "metapopulation" is helpful in describing the existence of "an ensemble of smaller populations connected by dispersing individuals [who] find it easier to accommodate the locals in adopting their speech habits than to maintain their own traits" (24–25). At the same time, an initially stable founder population can result in a maintained target variety by force of "generative entrenchment," "according to which what came earlier has a better chance of establishing deeper roots in a system than what was adopted later" (25). The cultural spaces that have emerged in Griffin can be analogized, albeit in more "shallow" time, to other processes of language development, for example, the emergence of Gullah and AAVE as described by Mufwene's "competition and selection principle." When the mill villages were first occupied by workers from other mills in the upper Piedmont regions and the regions in Appalachia, a certain continuity of cultural identity was established and maintained through effective social segregation of the discrete, boundaried spaces of the mills. These workers formed the founder population and their "ways" were the target to be acquired by anyone who wished to belong there. A prerequisite to "belonging" was to actually live in a village house and work in the local mill. Kinship was also an important factor, since most jobs were passed down through families and fellow workers did most of the training for different positions. The workers who came later, in periods of farm failures or during the Depression (when the mills continued to run full-time), were dispersing individuals who needed to accommodate to establish and maintain this life that was formed not by mere occupation, but by membership in a new kind of cooperative community. This community qualifies as a locality more identifiable by cultural allegiances than by geographical boundaries. Through accommodation, individuals become part of a local language community as well. Silverstein (1998, 404) elaborates on the definition of a local language community: "Locality must emerge from within, and is inherently only as stable as the processes that produce cultural concepts, semiotically both positive and negative, of anchored, or centered, and graduated inclusiveness of a distinctly imaginable collective experience of using a 'language,' a denotational code."

Meanwhile, the community outside the mill villages, that of the older, small-scale farmers, was undergoing changes as well. In the late nineteenth century, Jim Crow laws laid the groundwork for true racial segregation in the cities, but, as Mufwene (2000b, 18) points out, this kind of segregation did not work on small farms. Small farmers, both white and African American, shared similar heritage (as descendants of indentured servants, overseers, and slave owners) and continued to live and work in close contact. However, the divergence between these two speech varieties probably was beginning in the African American migrations northward and toward industry (both after the Civil War and again in the 1910s). After World War II, the separation was compounded by farm failures and white movement into new occupations, including the still racially segregated mills. In the 1980s, the mills began to close and move their operations to cheaper labor markets, taking away the institutional structures that had ordered much of Griffin's existence. These economic changes impacted cultural spaces and left a disjunctive terrain for the next generation. The villagers who knew the glory days of the mill are now undergoing what could be termed an identity crisis—a powerful example of this is Judy McKinley's (1999) intensely loyal memorial to her ex-neighbors, ex-coworkers, and kin only to emphasize the lost world.

EARLY NEW WORLD VARIETIES. British varieties of English had a large impact on New World varieties, and certain patterns have been helpful in establishing dialect boundaries (Kurath 1949; Pederson 1986–92). As mentioned above, early migrants to the Chesapeake colonies have been sourced to the general area of south and southwest England, and similarities in the distinct dialects have been noted. For example, Fischer (1989, 259)—following earlier dialectologists but employing less appropriate linguistic descriptors—claims that "virtually all peculiarities of grammar, syntax, vocabulary and pronunciation which have been noted as typical of Virginia were recorded in the English counties of Sussex, Surrey, Hampshire, Dorset, Wiltshire, Somerset, Oxford, Gloucester, Warwick or Worcester" (see also Mencken 1936). What Fischer characterizes as "peculiarities" are termed as such in contrast to the New England English that was spoken by migrants from the east of England (especially East Anglia) in the seventeenth century, characterized by "a harsh, high-pitched, nasal accent unkindly called the 'Norfolk whine'" (Fischer 1989, 57). The dialects in the New World South, influenced by south and southwestern English, were, on the other hand, "a soft, slow, melodious drawl that came not from the nose but the throat" (258). There was no pronunciation of /r/ (Kurath 1928, 14), but there was "embellishment" of vowel sounds in the form of "*ha-alf* for half, *gyarden* for garden, *ke-er* for care, *holp* for help, *puriddy* for pretty, *fuust* for first, *Aah'm* for I'm, *doo* for do, and the spectacular *wah-a-tah-mill-i-an* for watermelon" (Fischer 1989, 258). These features, and another mentioned by Fischer (*Ah be* for *I am*), were carried to the New World as part of "a dynamic process of linguistic selection and recombination" (262). As for the ensuing variation in the New World, he credits not only the archaism of certain features for their persistence, but also the additional layers of the linguistic ecology, including the influence of African speech and social factors such as class and education. Southern dialects, he concludes, evolved from dialects of the south and southwest of England into diverse and localized variants. One explanation for this divergence from the British sources is that the majority of this wave of migrants was either poor farmers or indentured servants from diverse backgrounds who ended up working together, interacting together on a regular basis, selecting similar features from a common feature pool, and developing a common colonial koiné (Mufwene 2000b).[4] From these farms, usually tobacco or cotton plantations, farmers migrated inward to the "hinterlands" of South Carolina, Georgia, and Alabama and established small-scale farming communities—towns like Griffin.

On the other hand, later migrations brought backcountry speech "developed from the 'northern' or 'Northumbrian' English that was spoken in the lowlands of Scotland, in the North of Ireland, and in the border counties of England during the seventeenth and early eighteenth century" (Fischer 1989, 654). It is significant that backcountry speech was first identified in "ethnic rather than regional terms, as Scotch-Irish speech" (652) because Appalachians would also often be thought of as an entirely different class. Travelers who recorded this variety had less favorable characterizations of its sound. Instead of the "soft, slow, melodious" sound of low country southern dialects, the backcountry speakers were said to "mangle and mutilate" English (652, n. 3). Later, this U.S. southern highlands influence would "become familiar throughout the western world as the English of country western singers, transcontinental truck drivers, cinematic cowboys, and backcountry politicians" (652), though this characterization overtly employs stereotypical generalizations that are not based on actual speakers. The pronunciation patterns that Fischer describes for this dialect highlight differences between low country and backcountry speech. For example, instead of lack of pronunciation of /r/, there is emphasized and even inserted /r/ pronunciation, as in *where* [hwar], *certain* [sartın], *narrow* [nærɚ], *widow* [widɚ], and *window* [wındɚ] (652). There is less vowel "embellishment" in the form of prolonging sounds, but there is more vowel tensing, as in *deaf* [dif], *poison* [paizın], *bush* [bʊsh], and *naked* [nɛkıd] (652). Other highlands features existed in common with low country speech, for example, *a-goin* 'going', *fixin* (about to do something), and *honey* (as a term of endearment).

Pederson (1986–72) identifies cultural areas within the South which inform the background of the farmers and mill villagers, and McDavid (1948) corroborates these social divisions with instances of linguistic differences, specifically using the pronunciation or vocalization of /r/ and monophthongization of /ay/ as examples.[5] "One's vowels," he claimed, "were clear markers of one's social standing" (1966, 34). These extremely salient features mark the boundaries between Pederson's South and South Midland cultural areas as well (Pederson 1986–92). Kretzschmar (1996), however, argues that dialect boundaries based on geographic settlement patterns are not so clear; this observation is true in large part because language is always being restructured (Mufwene 2000b, 25) and because the selection of features is not always exclusive (Mufwene 2001). This debate is related to the issue of how dialects in the United States have evolved. Kurath (1928, 19) has argued that Kentucky, Tennessee, southern Ohio, Indiana, Illinois and Missouri "received most of their early population from the Valley of Virginia and the Piedmont, where the Scotch-Irish predominated ... while the Cotton Belt of western Georgia, Alabama, Mississippi, Louisiana, and eastern Tennessee was settled very largely by the cotton-growers of the tidewater of VA and the Carolinas." He identified AAVE and Appalachian speech as "dialectal articulations" that have survived due to special circumstances. Although geographic isolation and similar heritage is a strong argument for the development of Appalachian English as a variety (Hazen 1996), Montgomery (1994b) also notes that some "Appalachian" features were available throughout the American South. For example, the presence of an Irish verb concord rule in Appalachian English may illustrate the tendency for speakers to select features belonging to more than one input source. Explanations of dialect convergence as "leveling" or simplification are also not so useful. Mufwene (2000b) joins Monttttgomery in arguing against this conception of koinéization as differences being "ironed out" in a contact situation. On the contrary, competition and selection from a larger pool of features is the process by which individual speakers effect language change.

INTERNAL MIGRATIONS AND LOCAL CONTACT SITES. As previously noted, Appalachians were the first to leave their land and sign on when textile mills began opening in the South in the very late 1800s, making them the founder population in the mill villages. Textile jobs were highly valued and passed on through family ties as well as from mill to mill connections (McDavid 1966; McKinley 1999, 30), and for several decades the mill villagers were almost as isolated as in the mountain villages they migrated from. Farm failures in the Piedmont areas reached bleak proportions after World War II, and farmers throughout the South filled the mills as they expanded. In this way, textiles were simultaneously associated with both failure and hope for a better life, and conflicting attitudes of pride and contempt polarized social relations between the two "classes."

Small-scale farmers, though not involved in large slave operations, did interact frequently with African Americans while the backcountry folk did so only rarely. A linguistic debate has long existed on the amount of influence African speech has had on southern white speech. The contact equation differed greatly between different groups of migrants and social classes. Large African populations were brought to the coastal plantations in the South, with much smaller African populations in the hinterlands. There were likely few Africans living in Appalachia before the middle of the twentieth century, and the African American population there now is still quite minimal. Fischer (1989, 264) claims that African influence on English varieties, even those in close contact with Africans, was secondary because settlers established varieties "before African slaves could possibly have had much impact on language." However, the earliest laborers in the colonies, both black and white, worked as indentured servants on cotton and tobacco plantations where they developed the same target variety of English together (Mufwene 2000b). These workers, who later moved inland, were the founder populations of farming communities throughout the South. As linguistic evolution has continued, social patterns have diminished contact between African Americans and whites, and most white varieties, excepting some southern varieties, are distinct from AAVE.

Despite some tendencies toward generalization and uniformity, speakers in social contact ensure heterogeneity of "mixed" Englishes (Krapp 1925). Kurath (1940) and Davis, McDavid, and McDavid (1969) argue that Southern whites and particularly Southern African Americans preserved certain archaic English features due to cultural patterns of predominantly rural, agricultural communities from which people were less likely to travel. However, the twentieth century was the scene of much mobility due to changing economic imperatives that came along with the decline of farming and the introduction of the steel, coal, and textile industries. Mufwene (2000a, 11) claims that all languages are "mixed" and rejects a restrictive family framework in favor of ethnographic research that reveals a fuller picture of the contact equation. Contact and conflict were very much a part of the Southern cultural landscape in the twentieth century and before. Although there was definitely a cultural differential between the North and the South, monolithic descriptions of a conservative Southern culture are inaccurate.

Bailey's (1997) description of data sources for older Southern and older SWVE varieties, based on the birth dates of various informants, leads him to argue that the current "stereotypical" Southern variety of English—Fischer's (1989, 652) language of "country western music, transcontinental truck drivers, cinematic cowboys, and backcountry politicians," in a broad sense—is a recent development that began in the late 1800s with the social changes and increased migrations following the Civil War. He bases these findings on the presence or absence of features that are, and are not, typical of current varieties of Southern English in a wide variety of print and speech samples. The current features do not occur much in the speakers born before 1875, only variably in speakers born before 1945, and almost invariably in speakers born after

1945. He assesses Kurath's geographic patterns as both right and wrong: a certain variety of SWVE did reflect original settlement patterns, but current SWVEs reflect more recent settlement patterns that occurred after the increased migratory patterns following the Civil War and then again after World War II. In Griffin, these general time periods coincide not only with the ends of wars, but also with economic changes. The first mill opened in Griffin in 1888; by 1945 the mills were booming and farm shares were in steep decline. The subsequent homecoming from World War II was an event that changed the economic and linguistic terrain.

The general pattern of speech in Griffin is the maintenance of distinctions in older speakers according to occupational communities, with more accommodation in younger speakers. This aligns with changing contact patterns reflected most dramatically by increasing instances of intermarriages in the loosening grid of status and proximity. What is interesting in this scenario is finding out which variants have been maintained and why they have been selected.

The older changes cited by dialectologists appear significantly in densely networked older people according to community. For example, absence of /r/ pronunciation and monophthongization of /ay/ (as in *Ah'm* for *I'm*) is an overwhelming statistic in older farmer speech in Griffin. On the other hand, rhoticity is predominant in mill villager speech, and even several examples of "intrusive" /r/ recur, including *Lisa* [lisɚ], *window* [wɪndɚ], and *Hawaii* [hawayɚ]. Distinctive Highlands verb constructions have also survived in mill villager speech, such as *he come in, she done finished, they growed,* and in emphatic double negatives (*he don't have none*).

## CONCLUSION

The linguistic contact equations of different regions of the South, then, varied greatly. In the large plantations, African varieties and European varieties were large factors. In the isolated Appalachian mountains, migrants from the borderlands of North England, Ireland, and Scotland brought their dialects through the valleys of

Virginia and the Piedmont to a relatively secluded and stable environment (Kurath 1928). In the interior cotton belt, specifically for this investigation in the mid-north, mid-western part of Georgia, a mix of cotton-growers from the tidewaters and a smaller number of African slaves made up a large part of the social ecology. Population ratios are important: a majority of African slaves populated the coastal areas, whites from the south and southwest of England dominated in the Piedmont areas, and whites from England's northern borderlands prevailed in the north Georgia mountains. In the twentieth century, the influx of cotton mills and mill workers from Appalachia and the frontier Piedmont regions into the interior cotton belt of Georgia (and parts of South Carolina and Alabama as well) added a new wrinkle to the contact equation of Griffin and other mill towns. As long as both occupations remained viable, however, the previous pattern of networks remained separate and relatively stable. Economic upheavals eventually broke up the institutional foundations upon which the separate communities were formed and produced a new scenario in which individuals were compelled to reevaluate former lines of group membership and identity. As linguistic geographies and life modes were renegotiated, oppositional and distinct speech patterns were recombined, thus changing the values of the variables in the restructuring equation of contact.

# 3. PHONOLOGICAL PATTERNS IN THE LINGUISTIC ECOLOGY OF GRIFFIN, GEORGIA

In this chapter I profile phonological patterns in the Southern White Vernacular English (SWVE) dialects spoken in Griffin. My objectives are to display quantitative findings of local phonological variables, describe patterns of change over apparent time from a sample that is one hundred years deep, and compare these patterns to trends found in other researchers' work. Factors that influence patterns of change and stability include salience, phonetic configurations (involvement in chain shifts, ease of articulation), and social variables (age, gender, community changes).

Table 3.1 shows that the occupational dialects of older speakers generally parallel particular regional dialects, that is, mill-villager speech is similar to Highlands speech, and farmer speech is similar to Lowland speech. This table is modeled after Wolfram, Hazen, and Schilling-Estes's (1999) comparison of features characteristic of subregional dialects. They also provide a category of "non-Southern" in a "purposely vague" sense in order to "group together features that are common to Midland and Northern dialect areas" (33). Wolfram, Hazen, and Schilling-Estes were most likely targeting this non-Southern field for input on the influence of geographically and culturally contiguous varieties. Kurath (1928), on the other hand, actually found similarities between the noncontiguous dialects of the Lowland South and eastern New England. He hypothesized that these kinships were based on similar dialectal roots in southern England. The distinctions in the New World, he claimed, are the result of different varieties of South England Standard and also of different regional dialects existent in Europe during the different waves of migration throughout the seventeenth, eighteenth, and nineteenth centuries. The possible influence of a "standard" in the past and at present will be further discussed in the context of recent influxes of non-Southerners and the effects of solidarity (chap. 5). The linguistic structures described here are

TABLE 3.1
Phonological Comparison of Griffin Features to Characteristic Regional Features

| *Structure* | *Mill Villager* | *Farmer* | *Southern Highland* | *Southern Lowland* | *Non-Southern* |
|---|---|---|---|---|---|
| SHIBBOLETHS | | | | | |
| Generalized /r/-dropping | | | | | |
| Absence of stress /r/ before C (*work* [wɜk]) | | + | | +/– | +/– |
| Absence of work-final /r/ (*her* [hə]) | | + | | + | +/– |
| Absence of stressed post-vocalic /r/ (*four* [foə]) | | + | | + | +/– |
| Absence of medial /r/ (*hired* [haəd]) | | | | | |
| Absence of unstressed /r/ (*Virginia* [vədʒɪnyə] | | + | | + | +/– |
| Specialized /r/-dropping | | | | | |
| /r/ absence intervocalically (*during* [dʊɪn]) | + | +/– | + | | +/– |
| /r/ absence after /θ/ and before /u/ and /o/ (*throw* [θo]) | + | | + | | |
| Intrusive /r/ and /t/ (*fellow* [fɛlr̩], *oncet* [wʌnst]) | + | | + | +/– | |
| /ay/ monophthongization | | | | | |
| Before voiced obstruents (*ride* [ra:d]) | + | + | + | + | |
| Before voiceless obstruents (*right* [ra:t]) | + | +/– | + | | |
| /ayr/ and /awr/ reduction (*tire, tower* [tar]) | + | | + | + | |
| THE SOUTHERN SHIFT | | | | | |
| Back Shift (*food* [fʉd]/[fʉ:d); *so* [sʌʉ]) | + | + | + | +/– | |
| Front Shift (*date* [da$^{i}$t]; *debt* [de$^{ʌ}$t]; *bit* [bi$^{ʌ}$t]; *beet* [bʌ$^{i}$t]) | +/– | | +/– | | |
| MERGERS | | | | | |
| /ɪ/~/ɛ/ merger before nasals (*pin/pen* [pɪn]) | +/– | + | + | + | |
| [ɑ/ɔ] merger, loss of upgliding [ɔ] (*cot/caught* [kɑt]) | | | | | + |

informed by a range of sources, including Bailey (1997), who hypothesizes that many nonstandard Southern features are RECENT developments; Pederson (1986–92), the traditional dialectologist research; Wolfram, Hazen, and Schilling-Estes (1999), who compare Southern isolate varieties, and my own data, based on occupational categories in Griffin. The work of Labov and his team of researchers is also closely examined with regard to defining the Southern Shift. Like most of the investigators cited here, I seek not only to compile the factual data, but also to imagine the scenario in which these results came to be from the combination and competition of diverse phonetic and social factors. Therefore, the dialects identified here are based on cultural constructs as well as regional delineations.

Several phonological features in Griffin are variable linguistic attributes that distinguish mill-villager and farmer speech patterns. They are described herein as belonging to one of three groups: shibboleths, the Southern Shift, and mergers.

## SHIBBOLETHS

Shibboleths are features that speakers themselves recognize as signaling inclusion in a particular social group. They are both negative and positive, since by marking inclusion they also entail exclusion. McDavid's early work in Greenville, South Carolina, revealed that two Southern features distinguish speakers not only as Southern, but also as belonging to a certain social group within the strata of Southern social hierarchies. These two features, /r/-lessness and /ay/-monophthongization, retain their status as social markers, though in differing degrees. /r/-lessness is a fading sound feature, while /ay/-monophthongization is still expanding.

ABSENCE, EMPHASIS, AND INSERTION OF /r/. One of the most salient markers of Lowland pronunciation is /r/-absence. Stereotypes of "plantation" speech employ this technique in syllable-final position (as in *brother* [brʌðə]) and in unstressed medial syllables (as in *yesterday* [yɛstədeˈ]). Less common are the instances of /r/-dropping sourced to Southern Highland dialects in intervocalic positions, more often after back vowels than front, as in *during* [dʊɪn], and before the back vowels [o] and [u], as in *throw* [θo] and *threw* [θu]. Wolfram, Hazen, and Schilling-Estes (1999) find these "more specialized patterns of /r/-dropping without general /r/-lessness" in Outer Banks English and link these occurrences to Southern Highland dialects. Drawing from their data, they hypothesize that "similar historical, social, and cultural situations may preserve the common linguistic heritage of two or more dialect areas even after centuries of separation" (44, 40).

In the Griffin dialects, the farmer speakers, especially the older generations, have very high rates of Lowland /r/-dropping, but almost no instances of Highland /r/-dropping. The older mill-villager speech aligns just as neatly on this salient feature, showing little Lowland /r/-dropping and clear instances of Highland /r/-dropping (with even some intrusive /r/). Intrusive /r/ is definitely receding, but remains a feature in the speech of older mill villagers. Alice, for example, calls the me *Lisa* [lisɚ], refers to *Hawaii* [hawayɚ], and "warshes" her clothes. Likewise, older mill villager Zelda demonstrates specialized /r/-dropping, generalized /r/-fullness, and even intrusive /t/:

> INTERVIEWER: They weren't around as much?
>
> ZELDA: Matt didn't come through [θu] the plant but once a year [wənstə yɪɚ].

Intrusive /r/ is practically nonexistent in the younger speakers and never appears in farmer speech. However, specialized /r/-dropping and intrusive /r/ are variable in older mill-villager speech. For example, in the following passage, Zelda's speech is predominantly /r/-full, but /r/-less in the word *hired*; intrusive /r/ occurs in *ruined* but not in *washcloth*; specialized /r/-dropping appears variably in *through*; and final [d] is devoiced to [t] in *ruined*, perhaps in a pattern related to intrusive /t/.

> PATTY: Yeah they're the run—run of the mill.
>
> INTERVIEWER: That's a funny phrase, isn't it? Run of the mill.
>
> ZELDA: Well we had—well they had towels that you could put up that way. If they didn't have a hole . . . if they had a hole in em that wasn't big enough to punch a finger THROUGH [θu], without

> pushing it THROUGH [θru]. You could let that go in the run of the mill. And we had WASHCLOTHS we could class that way. And see all the washcloths paid, they paid a different price. The run of the mill didn't pay as much as the others. And the nicer—nicer towels paid more. But you were sposed to be sure not let nothing go THROUGH [θu] that. And then later see, they had little inspectors ... that come around to your table and get in your work and look in it and see what was in it. They began—after them engineers come in there they HIRED JUST HIRED [haəd] so many different ones to go round and look at people's work and that's that's one thing that RUINED [rɚnt] the bleachery.

The concurrent alignment of intrusive /r/ with *r*-full speech is easily connected to historical dialects. /r/-fullness in Southern Highland dialects has long been established, and this trait also has been identified in borderlands dialects in the British Isles, Irish influence being one obvious source. On the other hand, /r/-lessness has historically been identified as a Southern prestige variant associated with early landowners and politicians. Although this opposition still exists in politics today, an interesting reversal is currently under way. For example, in a political crux between former Georgia governors—north Georgian Zell Miller and south Georgian Roy Barnes—curious alliances and dissonances emerged in which Miller, a popular Democrat who had filled a Republican's senate seat, was able to levy his persona as a viable commodity. Miller was a boundary-crosser in several ways: as a northern, hill-country Georgian, he brought a new "voice" to the governor's office both literally and figuratively. His /r/-full dialect bespeaks his nonplanter origins, and he moved from a Democratic affiliation to conservative alliances (with President Bush, among others). Miller was so popular that fellow Georgia senator Max Cleland found it necessary to defend himself in the *Atlanta Journal Constitution* against charges that he was "not like Miller" (Mark Serman, May 14, 2001, A1). Additionally, John Edwards, who ran for vice president in 2004, played up his mill-villager roots, albeit with a more polished accent. This new political presence reflects a shift in prestige notions—historically, Southern dialects associated with the old planter class dominated the political terrain.

Figure 3.1 displays the general trend of increasing rhoticization. Surprisingly, the patterning of /r/-pronunciation does not follow the typical paths of linguistic change in which female speakers lead the change and male speakers rapidly catch up. Instead, a criss-cross pattern is revealed, in which female farm speakers are quickly surpassed in /r/-pronunciation by their male counterparts in the middle-aged group and then take the lead again when the pattern recrosses in the younger group. This may be the result of males from farm backgrounds going to work in the mills. The stability of the mill speakers from middle-aged to younger groups reflects the "mellowing out" of /r/-pronunciation. As noted above, only the older mill speakers show instances of intrusive /r/ and Southern Highland /r/-deletion. However, perhaps the pattern of females leading and males quickly catching up does apply here, but across occupational categories. In fact, the expected track is seen in comparing the male farm speakers to the female mill speakers. One explanation for this pattern may lie in the kinds of intimate social contacts that occurred during this era. For instance, Annie, a middle-aged woman who grew up in the Highland mill village, is married to a man from a farm background whom she met in

FIGURE 3.1
General Increase of Rhoticization

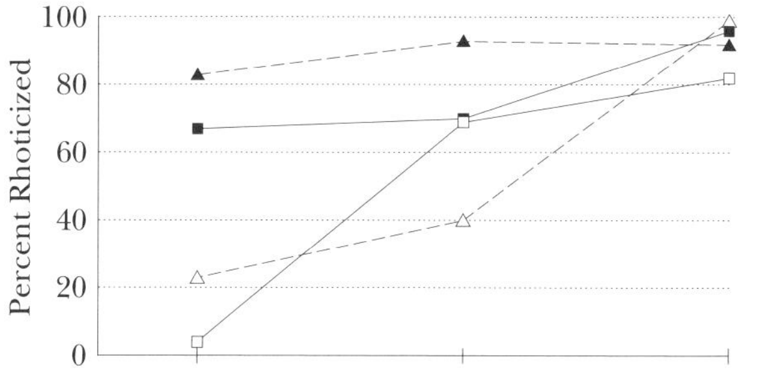

| | *Older* | *Middle-aged* | *Younger* |
|---|---|---|---|
| Female, mill | 83% | 93% | 92% |
| Male, mill | 67% | 70% | 96% |
| Female, farm | 23% | 40% | 99% |
| Male, farm | 4% | 69% | 82% |

Griffin's then newly consolidated high school. It is these types of intimate contact that triggered the dramatic changes that arose in the midst of an era when farm viability was being lost and the mills were operating at maximum capacity.

GLIDE DELETION. Monophthongization of /ay/, or glide deletion, is a salient marker of Southern speech that has been linked to both Highland and Lowland dialects. The shibboleth phrase *nice white rice* [na:s hwa:t ra:s] (glide deletion before unvoiced consonants) is a South Midland feature, where glide deletion also prevails in the environment before voiced consonants. This feature is variable in Kurath's South variety and in the farmer speech of Griffin, and it is not a norm found in non-Southern dialects. Each of these patterns are hypothesized to have advanced at different rates, with monophthongization in the voiced environment near completion by 1980 but ungliding in the unvoiced environment still widely variable (Bailey 1997). This variability is reflected in prestige patterns that are recorded as low prestige for ungliding in all environments (McDavid 1966), hence the status as a shibboleth that classes speakers as part of a certain cultural group. This pattern may also occur in some instances as hyperdialectalization. For example, Wendy, a newcomer to Griffin but an Atlanta native, has developed a new "accent" over the course of this study. Five years ago she married Peter, a man with roots in south Georgia who has strong ties to the agricultural community in Griffin. His speech includes monophthongization dominant in the voiced environment and variable in the unvoiced environment. Wendy's speech, however, demonstrates near categorical monophthongization in all environments, especially when speaking around her new friends.

Monophthongization of /ay/ has also been implicated in the *Vy* CHAIN SHIFT as an early movement in the Southern Shift. Other areas that participate in the Southern Shift, such as Southern England, Australia, Philadelphia, and the Outer Banks of North Carolina, participate in a tensing and raising of the variable /ay/, while SWVE is unique in its forward movement of /ay/ to [a:] (Labov and Ash 1997, 513). This movement putatively initiates a chain shift in which /iy/ (*beat*) and /ey/ (*bade*) fall and inglide, making room for /i/ (*bit*), /ɛ/ (*bet*), and /æ/ (*bat*) to tense and move up along the peripheral track (Labov 1996, 3). The Southern Shift is discussed in further detail below.

Ungliding of /ayr/ (*tire*) and /awr/ (*tower*) may be related to /ay/-monophthongization (Wolfram, Hazen, and Schilling-Estes 1999, 38), but in Griffin it also appears to be involved with variable /r/. For example, while Wolfram, Hazen, and Schilling-Estes describe this occurrence as prevalent in both Lowland and Highland varieties, the Lowland pronunciation of /ayr/ and /awr/ in Griffin is complicated by general /r/-loss. The farmer pronunciation of *tire*, for example, does not involve ungliding before /r/ because the /r/ is dropped in a final syllable. The resulting pronunciation is *tire* [taːə] or (rarely) [taː], as opposed to mill-villager pronunciation with unglided /ay/ but full rhoticization (*tire*, *tower* [tar]). Lowland speech, unlike the Highland variety, lexically distinguishes between *tire* [taːə] and *tower* [taːwə]. Variability of /r/ also affects the vowel in *there*, resulting in a Lowland patterns of *tire* [taːə], *tower* [taːwə], and *there* [ðeə] and a Highland pattern of *tire* [tar], *tower* [tar], and *there* [ðar].

The pattern of /ay/-monophthongization in Griffin is developing along with general Southern trends of more generalization across environments. This trend aligns with Bailey's findings of recent developments of Southern stereotypes. However, a distinction remains that ensures the viability of the shibboleth. Speakers who unglide in all environments are using a marked feature that identifies them as "Southern" or "country." In Griffin, this identity can take many forms: the Southern gentleman lawyer, for example, may unglide in voiced and word-final environments (especially with the lexical item 'I'), while the lower-class worker unglides in more environments. The case of Wendy, in turn, shows how accommodation may play a large role in the spread of this feature. Like many of her peers, her speech is augmented by the frequent instances of monophthongization that represent an imagined identity not always consonant with their forebearers' cultural histories.

When tracked by phonetic environment (figs. 3.2 and 3.3), /ay/-monophthongization patterns dramatically. All instances of glide deletion before voiced consonants and before null environments

FIGURE 3.2
Farmers' /ay/-Monophthongization by Sex and Following Phonological Environment

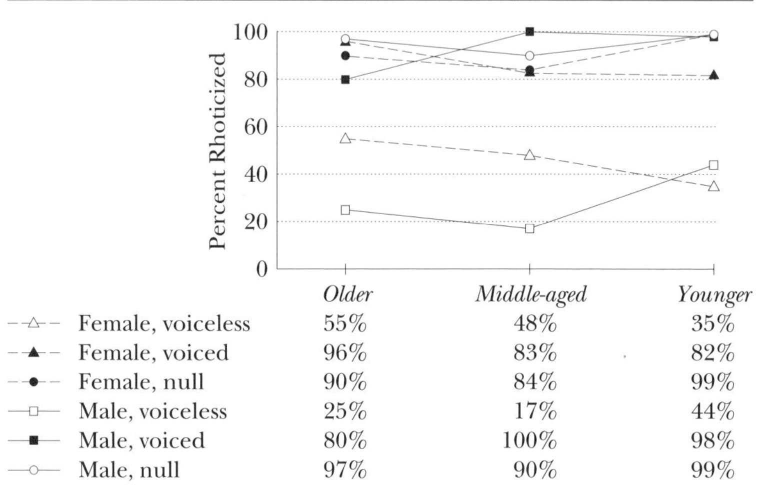


| | *Older* | *Middle-aged* | *Younger* |
|---|---|---|---|
| Female, voiceless | 55% | 48% | 35% |
| Female, voiced | 96% | 83% | 82% |
| Female, null | 90% | 84% | 99% |
| Male, voiceless | 25% | 17% | 44% |
| Male, voiced | 80% | 100% | 98% |
| Male, null | 97% | 90% | 99% |

FIGURE 3.3
Mill Villagers' /ay/-Monophthongization by Sex and Following Phonological Environment

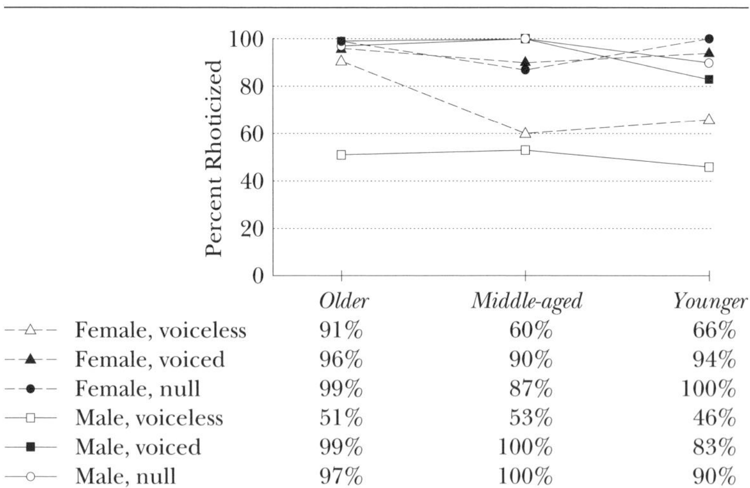


| | *Older* | *Middle-aged* | *Younger* |
|---|---|---|---|
| Female, voiceless | 91% | 60% | 66% |
| Female, voiced | 96% | 90% | 94% |
| Female, null | 99% | 87% | 100% |
| Male, voiceless | 51% | 53% | 46% |
| Male, voiced | 99% | 100% | 83% |
| Male, null | 97% | 100% | 90% |

rank 80% or above for all age groups in both occupations. Conversely, instances of glide deletion before voiceless environments rank 55% or below for all age groups of farmer speakers, with decreasing frequency for females but a sharp increase for males over apparent time (ungliding before voiceless consonants jumps from 17% for middle-aged farm males to 44% for younger farm males). For mill speakers, older females have equally high rates in this environment, and these frequencies decrease over time against the expected pattern of a change going to completion. Male mill speakers maintain stable variation at rates of 51% to 53% to 46%. Once again, the only parallel trajectories are the female mill speakers and male farm speakers. Both show a decrease of ungliding in the middle-aged group and an increase in the younger group that leads to the stable variation range of the male mill speakers (66% for the younger female mill speakers and 44% for the younger male farm speakers). Figures 3.4 and 3.5 offer a more transparent display of variation according to environment.

When males depart from the patterns of change led by their female counterparts (e.g., the farm males are not following the farm females), the most typical assumption is that there is some sort of covert prestige at work. However, the direction of dialectal

FIGURE 3.4
Farmers' /ay/-Monophthongization by Following Phonological Environment

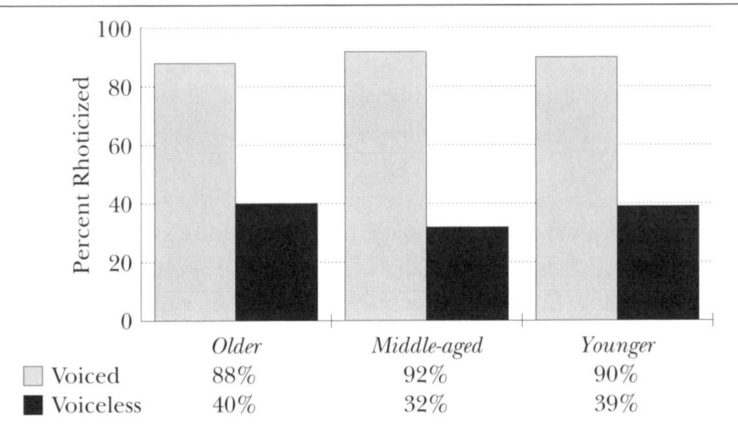

FIGURE 3.5
Mill Villagers' /ay/-Monophthongization by Following Phonological Environment

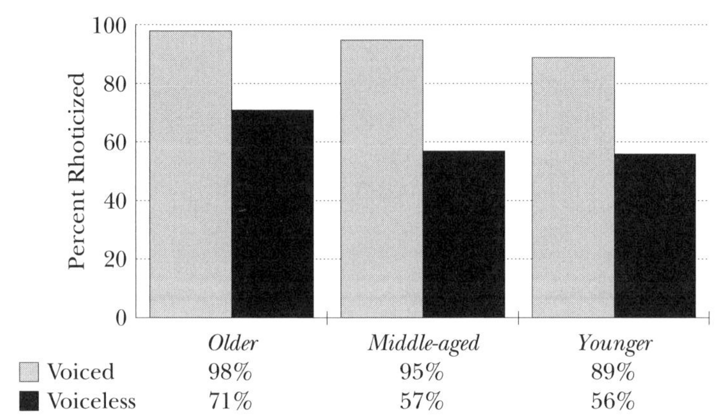


change in this case is toward a clearly demarcated realm of value-laden beliefs. Almost all of the males of all ages and occupations cited independence and self-sufficiency as desirable characteristics of farming. Additionally, the idea of a "country gentleman" has come up often in interviews with both mill and farm males. As Peter explains, with farming "you make your own hours, and you don't have to ask anybody what to do or how to do it." Land ownership, it would seem, still grants the same esteem it always has. In their interviews, females from mill backgrounds show more affinity to the community aspect of the fading mill villages. For instance, Kelly proudly asserts that all her generations are here, that her daughter has the same teachers she had, goes to the same skating rink she did, and so on. Deena struggles with still having to share her grandmother's house with her brother and mother, but admits that it is comforting to live in a village where everyone knows you and has known your family for generations. On the other hand, in answer to the question of what it is like to live in a mill village, Steve bluntly replies, "It sucks." Although he does not want to leave Griffin, he badly wants to leave the mill village, even if it means living in a trailer park. Billy has recently sold his parents' original bleachery village house to move them and himself into an upper-class neighborhood that none of them can really afford. The downward trajectory of mill-village economics is clearly evident to the males, while the females emphasize the remaining value of community.

These patterns indicate that the concept of "covert prestige," and perhaps even of "prestige," are too simplistic. In fact, the pattern that becomes evident from these seemingly disparate sets of data is a common one: both mill and farm males relate to the identity of an independent, self-sufficient person who lives on his own wits and his own land. Females, on the other hand, seem to value community and social commerce, which is reflected in their speech bending toward a shared dialectal space.

## THE SOUTHERN SHIFT

Following Labov, the Southern Shift can be described as a system of chain shifts responsible for a comprehensive sound change that covers not only the Southern region of the United States, but also southern England (especially Cockney), Australia, New Zealand, and South Africa (Feagin 1986b; Labov 1996; Labov and Ash 1997; Labov, Ash, and Boberg 2001). In the larger linguistic community, especially among linguists who are conducting dialect studies in the southern United States, the Southern Shift is not assumed to play a role of such totality (Bailey 1997; Wolfram, Hazen, and Schilling-Estes 1999). For example, Bailey acknowledges that the fronting of /o/ and lowering and retraction of /ey/ and /iy/ are chain shifts affecting a large regional area in the United States, but he does not include /ay/-monophthongization in this scenario due to chronological anomalies. These differences of assessment will be discussed in the following sections that focus on the front and back components of the Southern Shift. Labov outlines four major movements of the Southern Shift (only the first and second components of the Southern Shift are treated in depth here):[1]

1. V*w* fronting (marked as 5 and 6 on fig. 3.6). In the Southern states, the vowel classes /uw/ (*cooed*), /ow/ (*code*), and /aw/ (*cowed*) move forward to become phonetically [ʉ], [ʌʉ], and [æo], respectively (Feagin 1986b; Bailey 1997b). The vowel class /ʊ/ (*could*) may also

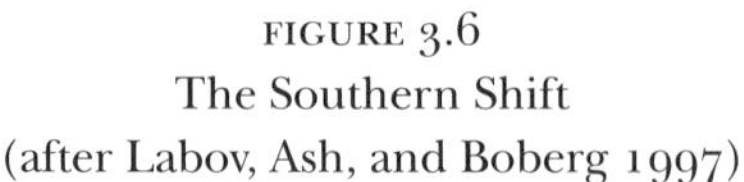

FIGURE 3.6
The Southern Shift
(after Labov, Ash, and Boberg 1997)

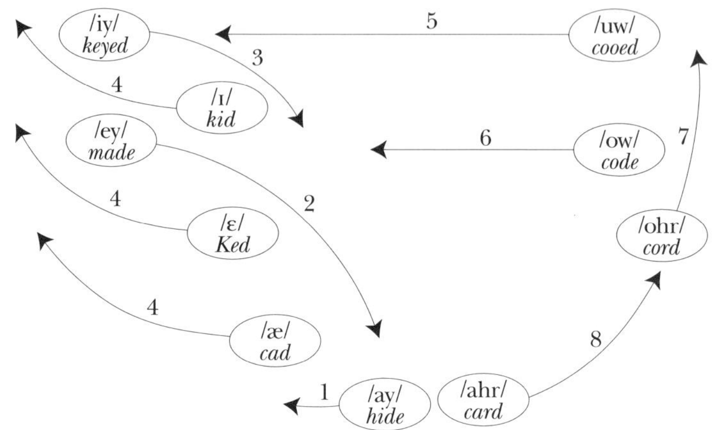


be involved in the shift. Both Fridland (2000) and Feagin (1986b) reported fronting with /uw/. While Feagin reported a mid-central character, Fridland found /uw/ and /ʊ/ in advanced speakers to front very early, "well in front of their /ʌ/ class" (270).

2. V*y* chain shift (marked as 2 and 3 on fig. 3.6). The dominant pattern in the Southern states is for /iy/ and /ey/ to lower and inglide on the nonperipheral track (see fig. 3.7) while /ay/ shifts forward and loses its glide to make room for the new /ey/. Examples of these sounds are found in the following word classes: /ay/, *bite* [baɪt] → [bat]; /iy/, *beet* [bit] → [bʌit]; and /ey/, *bait* [beit] → [bait]. This shift is closely interrelated with the fourth component, SHORT VOWEL TENSING; indeed, the two sound changes are often grouped together as the Front Shift, which "refers to the exchange in phonological space of tense and lax front vowels" (Feagin 1986b, 83).
3. V*h* raising (marked as 7 and 8 on fig. 3.6). This component of the Southern Shift is the backing and raising of the low and mid ingliding vowels. This chain shift is most common before /r/, as in /ohr/ (*tore* [toɚ]) and /ahr/ (*card* [kɔɚd]) and is sometimes characterized as a merger. Bailey (1997) cites Kurath and McDavid (1961) and Thomas and Bailey (1992) for the merger of /ɔr/ and /or/ in which *for* becomes [foɚ]. Bailey further notes that this merger has long competed with another merger between /ɔr/ and /ɑr/ (*lord/lard* = *lard*):

FIGURE 3.7
Illustration of Peripheral and Nonperipheral Tracks of Vowel Movement (Labov 1994, 177)

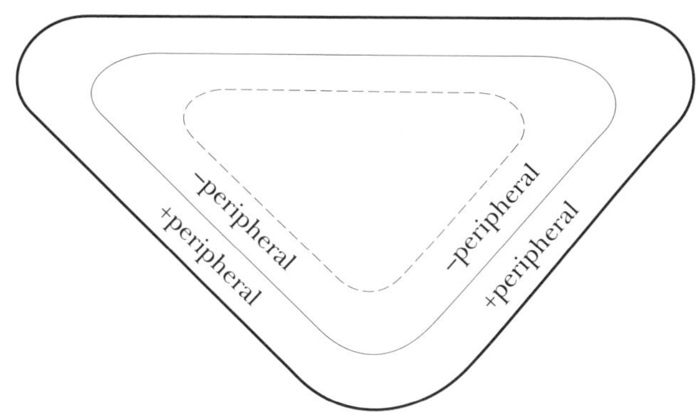


> For more than half a century the two mergers competed both with each other and with the three-way distinction, but the /ɔr/-/ɑr/ merger has lost out to the /ɔr/-/or/ merger just as the three-way distinction has. [Bailey 1997, 263]

Mergers are discussed further below.

4. SHORT VOWEL TENSING (marked as 4 on fig. 3.6). The short vowels notated as /ɪ/ (*bit*), /ɛ/ (*bet*), and /æ/ (*bat*) move up into the phonetic space vacated after the V*y* chain shift. Thus *bit* [bɪt] → [biᵊt], *bet* [bɛt] → [beᴧt], and *bat* [bæt] → [beæt]. In SWVE, these vowels lengthen and develop inglides to become members of the set /ih, eh, æh/ (*idea, yeah, salve*), which shows up in words like *beer* and *bear* in non-rhotic dialects (Labov and Ash 1997, 513–14).

Following the general trend of investigative focus, this discussion concentrates on the Front and Back Shifts of the Southern Shift, including /iy/, /ey/, /ɪ/, and /ɛ/ in the Front Shift and /uw/, /ow/, and /aw/ in the Back Shift. The third and fourth developments of the shift are in large part projections of the shift at an advanced stage. This stage of development is probably premature since the very status of the vowel changes as a chain shift are still debatable. In the larger linguistic community, especially among linguists who are conducting dialect studies in the southern United States, the sound changes implicated in the Southern Shift are not assumed to interrelate quite so clearly (Bailey 1997; Wolfram, Hazen, and Schilling-Estes 1999; Fridland 2000).

CRITICAL BACKGROUND. Fridland (2000, 268) critiques Labov's application of "universal patterns" and questions the validity of classifying vowel changes as participants in a chain shift. Her data extend Labov's and Feagin's coverage to Memphis, an urban locale in the South Midland dialect area (the other studies were conducted in the lower South in smaller to mid-size cities, Birmingham and Anniston, Alabama, respectively). In her results, Fridland confirms vigorous shifting of the /ey/ class and some movement in the /ɛ/ class but little to no participation in the other part of the Front Shift, that of the /iy/ and /ɪ/ classes. In the back vowels, /uw/ and /ʊ/ are well advanced in forward shifts and also, along with /ow/, falling. Memphis speakers also exhibit a tendency to centralize, demonstrated by fronting and raising of the diphthongs /aw/ and /ay/. The vowel class /ɔ/ is falling and fronting into an /ɔ/~/ɑ/ merger, which confirms Feagin's (1986b) report from Anniston. Fridland (2000, 281) hypothesizes (contra Labov) that the Back Shift is older than the Front Shift since Memphis speakers with limited Front Shift have advanced Back Shift, and the Back Shift is "embedded in all the older speakers' systems more consistently than the shifts in the front vowels." Also, the Front Shift is weaker in younger speakers while the Back Shift is more vigorous. Fridland found several sound changes not represented in Labov's model, including /ɔ/~/ɑ/ low back merger, fronting of /ʊ/ class, falling in the /uw/, /ʊ/, and /ow/ classes, and raising of /aw/ and /ay/. She concludes that "there does not appear to be a unitary cohesive shift tying together the entire system" (283).

Feagin (2000) explores these contrary results and offers a few possible explanations. First, she argues that the two data samples are not comparable because Memphis is not in the same dialect area and that it may even be considered an anomaly akin to New Orleans due to its status as a diverse contact site as a large urban center on the Mississippi River. Second, Feagin questions the comparability of the data samples based on differing methodology: Fridland's data were obtained from reading passages and word lists, not conversational data. Also, Fridland's age depth is not as deep as Feagin's, whose oldest speakers were born in the 1880s. Finally, Feagin contrasts the demographic character of Memphis and the Alabama cities, noting that the direction of changes may be progressing from small to large places (in reverse of the gravity model). If such was the case, then Memphis might be behind Alabama in the Southern Shift, especially if, as Feagin hypothesizes, the changes are from below both in social hierarchy and below consciousness. One last possibility is that if these vowel sounds are perceptible, they may be regarded as "country" or small town and thus avoided by big city dwellers.

The data from Griffin have much to contribute to this debate. Like Feagin's research, it is based on conversational data from a small town with a reasonable age depth, and like Fridland's community, it describes a contact site. However, this contact site instantiates the situation that so many twentieth-century sound changes have been attributed to: Griffin's contact equation stems from a definite move toward urbanization caused by the increase of industry. Ecologically, the linguistic and cultural mix is not as diverse as a town on the Mississippi River, but rather, until recently, population segments could be clearly identified along the farmer/mill worker juxtaposition.

Griffin is also a potential midpoint between Fridland's and Feagin's data points since it is a medium-sized town versus the small town of Anniston, Alabama, and the large city of Memphis. If, as Feagin claims, the shift is moving from small towns to large towns, then the speakers in this Griffin sample should be participating. Although this group of speakers does not strictly reflect social hierarchies like those visible in Anniston, it is possible to speculate on the direction of preference for different groups. One complication that is avoided here is the question of whether or not the shifts are perceptible. I have employed several transcribers to note only those tokens that are clearly audible to them as being part of the dialect shift. Transcribers were trained by comparing recordings of nonshifted tokens to shifted tokens that were verified by acoustic analysis beforehand. Therefore, all tokens of shifted vowels in this data are verified as audibly perceptible.

*Vy* CHAIN SHIFT (THE FRONT SHIFT). Labov and Ash (1997) describe the *Vy* chain shift as a continuation of the effects the Great Vowel Shift has had on diphthongs of the tense mid-vowels. Bailey (1997) includes the lowering and retracting of /ey/ as part of the Southern Shift and finds that it began to emerge in the 1875–1945 period, becoming established in the 1945–80 period. The co-occurrence of the separate movements, if not the codependence, is thus chronologically compatible with general findings. Monophthongization of /ay/ occurs at roughly the same time periods as this part of the Southern Shift (Bailey 1997, 262). Once /ay/ has moved forward and lost its glide, then /ey/ has space to lower and retract. Since "the downward trajectory of /ey/ is dependent on the completeness of the monophthongization of /ay/ ... it stands to reason that the speakers who show the extreme form of [/ey/ lowering] will be a subset of those who monophthongize" (Labov, Ash, and Boberg 1997, 12). Furthermore, the movement of /iy/ is dependent on the completion of the movements of /ay/ and /ey/, and the reversal of /ɪ/ (*bit*) and /iy/ (*beat*) is "considerably less frequent" (13). While Labov, Ash, and Boberg found /ey/ lowering in nine speakers "concentrated in a coherent area ... that includes most of the Appalachian area and the Piedmont, excluding the Coastal South," they found /iy/ and /ɪ/ reversal in only three speakers in the same area, all located at the periphery along the Appalachian Mountains (13). These shifts are not represented in the coastal Southeast, primarily because of its characteristic laxing of long high and mid-nuclei, which maintains a greater (Cartesian) distance between /ey/ and /ay/. As noted above, the /ɪ/ and /iy/ reversal is even rarer in the South Midland (Fridland 2000).

Figure 3.8 shows the averaged trends of the combined variables of the Front Shift in Griffin. The most obvious pattern that appears is the spike in usage by mill men and farm men. As in previous data, this change occurs in the middle-aged group. Chronologically, this period corresponds to the consolidation of Griffin's separate high schools, which brought together mill kids and farm kids at a time when more people from both occupations began attending school beyond the seventh grade. This also parallels the decline of farming after Roosevelt's reforms had taken their toll and the boll weevil

FIGURE 3.8
Frequency of Front Shift
(combined average frequencies of shifted /iy/, /ɪ/, /ey/, and /ɛ/)

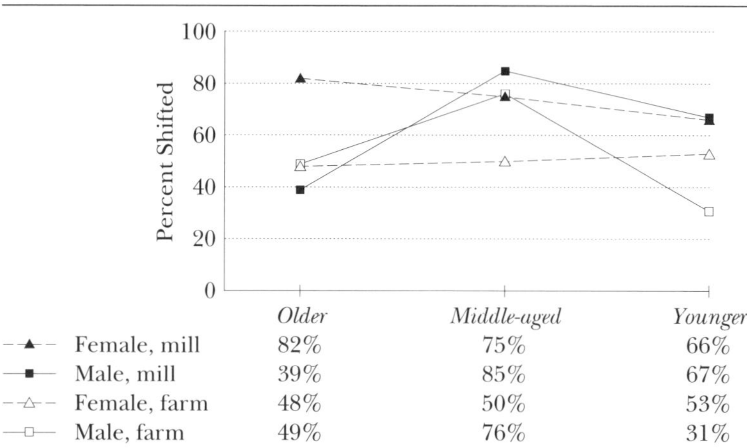


| | *Older* | *Middle-aged* | *Younger* |
|---|---|---|---|
| Female, mill | 82% | 75% | 66% |
| Male, mill | 39% | 85% | 67% |
| Female, farm | 48% | 50% | 53% |
| Male, farm | 49% | 76% | 31% |

and overfarming had exhausted the cotton fields. Furthermore, this era of the 1950s aligns with Bailey's claim that changes such as /ey/ lowering and retracting became established in the 1945–80 period. Mill women show stable variation during this time and then a gradual decrease in the younger group. However, farm women show little change, stable variation, and not much participation in the shift. Why aren't they participating? Farm women I talked to did not go to the mills, either in marriage or work or social life. In the middle-aged group, where Front Shift tokens are plentiful for the others, the farm women show a lack of linguistic involvement. In fact, lack of social involvement may have indeed been a factor. Louise and Barbara both found town jobs, and Donna is actually still a farmer. Conversely, the farm men did move both socially and in occupation: William married Annie, who grew up in a mill village, and Mitch and Hubert both found work at the mill.

Examining this shift in Griffin is informative since this is a good example of speakers in a contact situation where various factors play a role in feature selection, including identity, regional origin, and phonetic relationships. For example, it is well documented that loss of glide occurs first and most frequently before voiced consonants and word-finally. Labov, Ash, and Boberg (1997, 12) go so far as to characterize /ay/-monophthongization before voiced consonants as "the unmarked form throughout the South [that] defines the region." On the other hand, ungliding before voiceless consonants, as in the shibboleth phrase *nice white rice,* is still in progression (Bailey 1997) and presumably marked. Correlated with McDavid's (1966) data in which monophthongization in the unvoiced environment was extremely rare, the same feature before unvoiced consonants now "is well known to be a socially marked feature" (Labov, Ash, and Boberg 1997, 12). So, the patterning of social identity affects the Southern Shift because some speakers will completely move /ay/ to make way for /ey/ and /iy/ lowering, while others will only go halfway, and others will participate even less. As seen above, /ay/-monophthongization has not generalized in all speakers and probably, due to its salience as a "Southern" marker, never will. If Labov, Ash, and Boberg's assertion concerning the prerequisite of completed /ay/ shift for the /ey/ shift and its pursuants is stringent, then the Front Shift may have encountered a serious roadblock. Is it possible that the cycle could lock up—due to highly marked feature—and move in reverse? Another example from Griffin is that of /ey/ lowering, which is now characteristic of speakers who have the social correlates of less education and lower income. However, participation in /ey/ lowering and the rest of the front shift was heightened during a time of solidarity, the 1950s and 1960s, when teenagers from the separate worlds of mill villages and farms came together and individuated themselves from the previous generation through inclusivity. During that time, /ey/ lowering progressed even without speakers fully completing the /ay/-shift. This feature also plays a role as a marker of Southern identity and may reflect increasing solidarity among all whites—but especially among working-class whites—under the threat of racial desegregation. The mill/farm distinction in Griffin thus affords insight to the intersection between sound shifts in phonetic space and dialect shifts in cultural space.

*Vw* FRONTING (THE BACK SHIFT). Although this sound change is characterized as "the oldest and the most widespread aspect of the Southern Shift" (Labov and Ash 1997, 513), it is also said to occur later in the V*y* chain shift. For example, V*w* fronting of /uw/ and /ʊ/ (resulting in *food* [fʉd]) is identified as the fifth stage of the chain shift, occurring after monophthongization of /ay/ (the first stage) and the ensuing shifts of /iy/, /ey/, /ɪ/, /ɛ/, and /æ/ (Labov 1996, 3; Labov, Ash, and Boberg 1997, 11). Other evidence shows that /uw/ fronting developed before 1875 and went to completion in the 1875–1945 period, while /ay/-monophthongization began in the 1875–1945 period and has still not gone to completion (Bailey 1997, 262). Labov notes that "the fronting of /uw/ (and /ʊ/) is reported as appearing variably in the earliest period, before 1875, and consistently from 1875 onward, and appears to have been TEMPORALLY the earliest stage of the Southern Shift" [my emphasis] (Labov, Ash, and Boberg 1997, 11). However, stages 2 (/ey/ lowering) and 6 (/ow/ fronting) show "the same history" as stage 1 (/ay/-monophthongization) (11). This configuration is asynchronous in that temporal changes do not match with the order proposed for the chain shift, that is, a sound change can be progressing before it becomes engaged in the overall chain shift. Labov, Ash, and Boberg admit that "the temporal sequences are not as well established as for the Northern Cities shift" (11). Bailey differentiates between sound changes that are usually grouped together as parts of the Southern Shift and further specifies chronological order:

> The absence of constriction in post-vocalic and syllabic /r/, intrusive /r/, upgliding /ɔ/, and long offglides of /æ/ before /g/, /n/, and voiceless fricatives all appear in data on mid-19th century SAE [SWVE].... However, the fronting of /au/, the "Southern Shift" (i.e. the lowering and retraction of /e/ and /i/ and lowering and fronting of /o/), monophthongization of /ay/ before voiced obstruents [before unvoiced obstruents came even later], and the Southern Drawl, along with the *pen/pin* merger, all seem to be features that either emerged during the last quarter of the 19th century or became widespread during that time. [Bailey 1997, 263]

His definition of the Southern Shift includes only those shifts that can be chronologically and phonetically accounted for, but he notes that the classification of these vowels is difficult. The fronting of /u/ and /ʊ/ probably began in the nineteenth century but seems to have continued in the twentieth century to a position where /u/ is further front than the mid-vowel it initially moved to; that is,

Bailey's data show that /u/ is now a front rounded vowel (1997, 263). Following Bailey, I will examine this feature as a special case. Although it appears that /u/ and /ʊ/ fronting does play a role in the V*y* chain shift, the chronology of its emergence is still unclear. Furthermore, the dual nature of this feature's evolution may affect the viability of this feature in the process of competition and selection.

In Griffin, V*w* fronting is common in both mill and agricultural communities and in all age groups (see fig. 3.9). This preponderance suggests that the feature was in wide use in the early twentieth century and that it has prospered in the different cultural ecologies where other features remain distinct. Many of the farmers, including older speaker Edward and his niece Louise, pronounce lexical items such as *school* and *pool* extremely fronted so that the [l] fades and even disappears, as in *school* [skʉː]. On the other hand, Patty, an older mill worker, fronts these items and also fronts [ʊ] to [u], as in *full* [ful] (echoing Fridland's findings of a vigorously advanced /ʊ/ front shift). Her husband, Alfred, pronounces *July* as [dʒjʉˈlaː] with emphasis on the first syllable and the vowel fronted with a slight glide. The other vowel classes that are part of V*w* fronting in

FIGURE 3.9
Frequency of Back Shift
(combined average frequencies of shifted /uw/, /ow/, and /aw/)

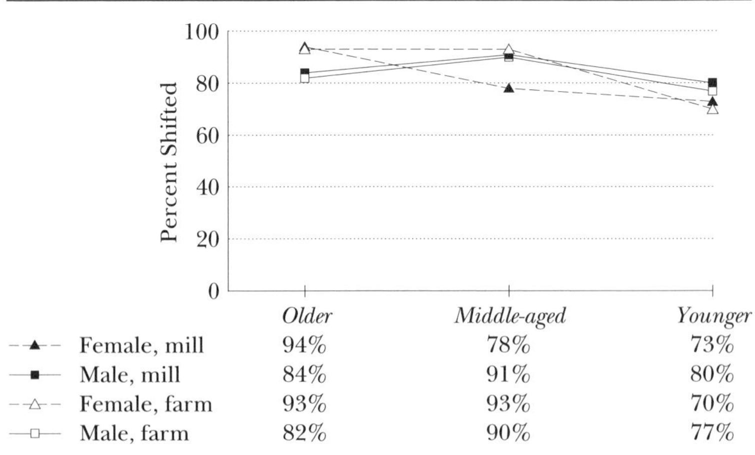

the Southern Shift, /ow/ (*code*) and /aw/ (*cowed*), do not pattern as categorically, although /aw/ is common in both occupational categories of speakers. *Code* [kʌ°d] and *cowed* [kæ°d] are common in mill-worker speech and in the speech of younger Griffinites in both occupational categories, but not a norm in farmer speech of the older and middle generations.

Although the Back Shift is still evident in the younger group of speakers in Griffin, it is not as vigorous as in the Memphis data Fridland (2000) describes. In fact, both the Front Shift and the Back Shift appear to be receding rather than progressing, a finding that contradicts Feagin's prediction that the changes are spreading from small to large towns. If the Back Shift is older, as Bailey claims, and became established in the 1945–80 period, then regression in younger speakers is perhaps not such a surprise. However, the Southern Shift is projected to be more of a long-term change, reading from Labov's linking of it to the Great Vowel Shift. There is evidence of /uw/, /ʊ/, and /ow/ falling, as Fridland has found, and this seems to be an incipient change in Griffin, since the extreme fronting of the Back Shift occurs in the middle-aged groups of speakers. While some alternatives to /ay/-monophthongization, such as centralizing, occur in younger speakers, the other movement that Fridland found, that of /aw/ fronting and raising, does not appear to be a trend. Fridland also recorded centralizing instances of /ɔ/~/a/ merger, which does not show up in the Griffin data (discussion follows below).

## MERGERS

Mergers are interesting because they contrast with the cooperative nature of chain shifts, and they are often lexically based. While many linguists call mergers "highly salient," the very nature of a merger is that vowel sounds are NOT very distinctive and are allowed to move to the same phonetic space instead of differentiating. Furthermore, competition between merging sounds is an equally confounding concept: do they move to a neutral point or does one of the competitors lose by moving to the space of its competitor?

THE *PIN/PEN* MERGER. The merger of /ɪ/~/ɛ/ before nasals, in which [ɛ] raises to [ɪ], as in *pin/pen* [pɪn] and *him/hem* [hɪm], is a well-attested feature of Southern dialects in both white and African American vernaculars (Bailey and Maynor 1989; Butters 1989; Brown 1991). Many linguists report it as being highly salient and thus typical of Southern speech, but perhaps this is only true for those who still have the distinction. As a Southerner, for instance, I do not notice distinctions when I hear them, probably a result of having usually relied on context and modifiers to differentiate lexical items (e.g., *safety pin, ink pen, straight pin, bowling pin*). This merger is a recent feature, developing in the 1875–1945 period and going to completion by 1980 in Texas (Bailey 1997, 266) and by 1930 in Tennessee (Brown 1991). Drawing on data from the Linguistic Atlas of the Gulf States, the Linguistic Atlas of the Middle and South Atlantic States, and the Tennessee Civil War Veterans Questionnaires, Brown shows that the raising of [ɛ] before nasals expanded rapidly and became predominant in the early twentieth century. She finds that the sound change patterned in classic configurations, such as females leading the change, greater occurrence in less-educated speakers, and diffusion from rural-to-urban regions that strongly correlates with urbanization. Brown (1990, 1991) reports no appreciable ethnic differences between white and African American speakers. Bailey's (1997) survey compares twentieth-century data with data gathered from the last quarter of the nineteenth century and finds similar patterns in speakers across a broad range of time and geography. He concludes, "The convergence of these sources of evidence makes it quite clear that the spread of the *pin~pen* merger in the South occurred long after the colonial period and cannot be traced to settlement history" (257). Brown concurs that the merger's "spread can hardly be accounted for by identifying its origins," but, unlike Bailey, she asserts that the variant pronunciations

> were probably brought from Britain by the original settlers of the Atlantic seaboard. Most likely /ɛ/ as in *pen* predominated in the English of the early settlers, but /ɪ/ was significantly represented by both English and Irish speakers of little education, who retained it as an insular, rural, relic variable feature when they settled in North Carolina and Tennessee. [311]

She credits the rise of Southern industry as the instigating factor for the merger's rapid diffusion and completion and characterizes the /ɛ/ variant as a "rural relic" (311). Griffin models this contact situation well: textiles served as a people mover throughout the southeast. The first migrants to textile towns were people living in the interior areas of North Carolina, South Carolina, and north Georgia, that is, poor areas that were close to the new textile sites. Skilled workers, they formed the founder populations of many mill villages in the South. The next migrations were from neighboring counties where farming had become untenable. Also helped along by its extreme ease of articulation and not having much to sacrifice in the move, the *pen/pin* merger took place quickly and quietly, moving first through the mill population (the change occurring in the middle-aged group) and one generation later in the farm population (see figs. 3.10 and 3.11). In fact, the only really noticeable effects occur when certain speakers push the /ɛ/ variable even further to the first part of an /iy/ diphthong. Labov (1996, 2) writes that the /ɪ/~/ɛ/ distinction before nasals was maintained in the South Midland area, but that region is now experiencing variation in what may be the spread of the merger northward and westward. This "highly salient" merger is also commonly found in contemporary SWVE, including Ocracoke English, Harkers English, Outer Banks

FIGURE 3.10
Frequency of the *pin~pen* Merger, Farmers

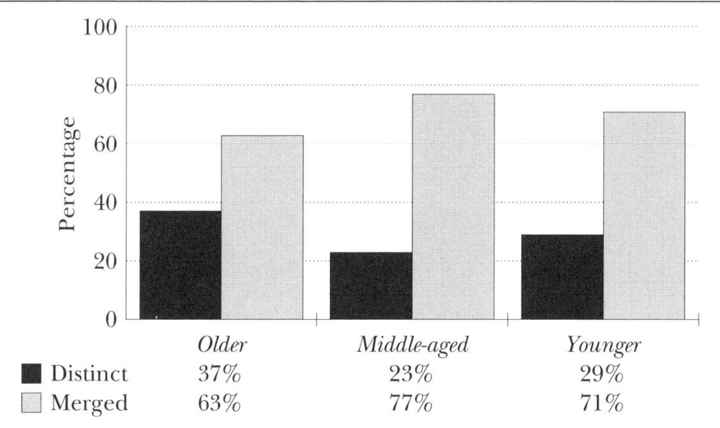

FIGURE 3.11
Frequency of the *pin~pen* Merger, Mill Villagers

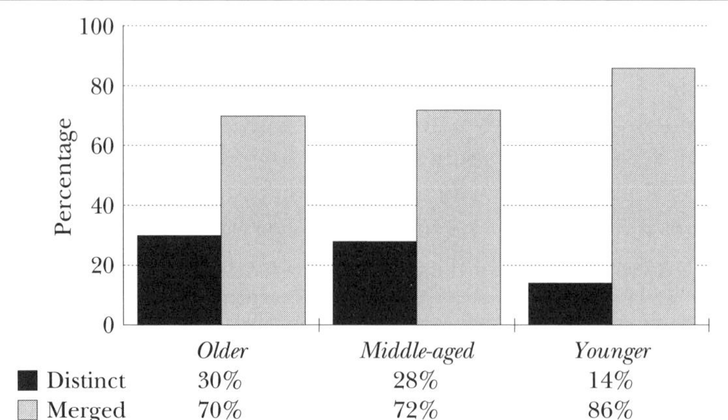


English, Highland South, and Lowland South (Wolfram, Hazen, and Schilling-Estes 1999, 38–39). The only small pockets of Southern nonmerging are found in rural areas and in isolated areas, as in the mountainous region north of Knoxville (Brown 1990, 58).

As for the mechanism of this sound change, Brown concludes that it is not part of a chain shift, but both merger-by-approximation or drift and merger-by-transfer. It is phonetically gradual, proceeds across a continuum, affects all relevant environments simultaneously with Neogrammarian regularity, and shows no evidence of lexical diffusion. The phonetic continuum of tensing and raising (/ɛ/→/ɛ$^{\wedge}$/→/ɪ$^{\wedge}$/→/ɪ/) follows Labov, Yaeger, and Steiner's (1972) predictions that vowels before (front) nasals become tense and that peripheral or tense vowels rise. The sound change is probably not part of a chain shift since there is no indication of Southern raising of /æ/ to /ɛ/ or /ɪ/ to /i/. Also (citing Labov, Yaeger, and Steiner 1972, 39), Brown recalls that "chain shifts rotate features and preserve distinctions; mergers neutralize features and lose distinctions." Brown also found a phonetic hierarchy in which the merger occurs most often in monosyllables with no consonant clusters (e.g., *ten, pen, hen*) and least often in polysyllables with consonant clusters (e.g., *twenty*). Since the sound change is a phonetically gradual process, moves along a continuum, is sociolinguistically constrained, and results in one of the original phonemes, Brown classifies it as a "partial merger" (1990, 116) that does not exactly fit into either category of merger-by-transfer or merger-by-drift or by approximation.

In Griffin, a few older men maintain the /ɪ/~/ɛ/ distinction, perhaps confirming Brown's assessment of the influence of industry. Older mill-villager speech is variable, and younger speech across occupations shows the near totality of this merger. The speech of Patty and Alfred, older mill villagers, exhibits some apparent gender variation in which Patty's speech shows almost complete loss of the distinction while Alfred's speech maintains variation. This pattern is confirmed by another older mill-villager couple, Paul and Zelda.

So, finally, the question of competition and selection concerning mergers involves just as many variable factors as any other kind of change. One possible motivation for the *pin/pen* merger may be economy. This feature analysis was the only instance in which it was necessary to have speakers read from word lists. The ideal target words are homonyms, and they don't occur very often in natural conversation. In fact, it is exceedingly rare to naturally come upon instances of both *pin* and *pen* or *tin* and *ten* in a single 45-minute conversation. Therefore, the motivation is not merely to be able to distinguish homonyms: the most common occurrences of /ɛ/, in fact, occur in unique lexical items such as *when, been, twenty*, and *remember*. Ease of articulation is another factor influencing change. Since the potential occurrence of homonyms is not great, perhaps it is a matter of not really giving up much and gaining ease of articulation. Is the loser really moving to its competitor's site, or is the competitor being invaded? At any rate, most speakers, including this linguist, seem to have submitted peacefully, blissfully unaware of the coup.

THE *COT/CAUGHT* MERGER. The loss of distinction between variables /a/ (*cot*) and /ɔ/ (*caught*) is reported to meet with "considerable resistance" in SWVE (Labov 1996, 2). It is the only unconditioned merger in North American dialects, which means that it affects phonemes wherever they appear, regardless of environment (1). For example, this merger collapses distinctions between pairs such as *Don/Dawn*, *cot/caught*, and *hock/hawk*. Even though the range of this merger is quite broad, it is rarely reported in the South—for example, it is not found on the Outer Banks (Wolfram, Hazen, and Shilling-Estes 1999) nor in the data from the Tennessee Civil War Veterans Questionnaire, the Linguistic Atlas of the Middle and South Atlantic States, the Linguistic Atlas of the Gulf States, and *Shorter Oxford English Dictionary* (Bailey 1997). However, a competitor of this merger exists in the South between [ɑ] and [ɔ], which is replacing the older Southern feature of upgliding /ɔ/ (Bailey 1997). In other words, these vowel classes are definitely merging, and there are perhaps more than one form of merger to choose from. The "Southern norm" of upgliding /ɔ/ is a low back upgliding vowel (*hawk* [hɑ$^{<o}$k]) that was typical of the Southeast, "including the Atlantic coastal South and the Piedmont areas of the Carolinas southward through Georgia and Alabama" (Wolfram, Hazen, and Schilling-Estes 1999, 38). The merger, however, is a recent development that has just begun in the 1945–80 period but has expanded so rapidly that the upgliding /ɔ/ feature has already disappeared in younger speakers and been replaced with [ɑ] (Bailey 1997, 266). However, in Birmingham, Labov and Ash (1997) find a majority of upgliding /ɔ/ (*caught*) (Labov's /oh/): out of 22 tokens in the speech of an 18-year-old woman, 14 were upglides, 2 were inglides, and 7 were monophthongs. No comparisons were made to /ɑ/ (*cot*), so it is yet to be seen whether a merger of these vowels is taking place in that city. In Griffin, upgliding /ɔ/ is very strong in the older and middle-aged groups of speakers from both mill and farm backgrounds. However, the younger speakers are participating in a change. While there are very few instances of /ɑ/ in Griffin—Tom says it once in the word *online*, and Kelly uses it in the filler word *because*—younger speakers are dropping upgliding /ɔ/ usually in favor of non-gliding /ɔ/. Figures 3.12 and 3.13 show that farm speakers are slightly more likely to drop upgliding /ɔ/ than mill speakers, but the two populations look indistinguishable overall. Although this distinction appears to be holding in Griffin, there are enough random instances of /ɑ/ to indicate that the merger Bailey has found in Texas may be beginning here.

Tillery's (1989) thesis examines this sound change in Texas, drawing from the Linguistic Atlas of the Gulf States, Phonological

FIGURE 3.12
Decreases in Upgliding /ɔ/, Farmers

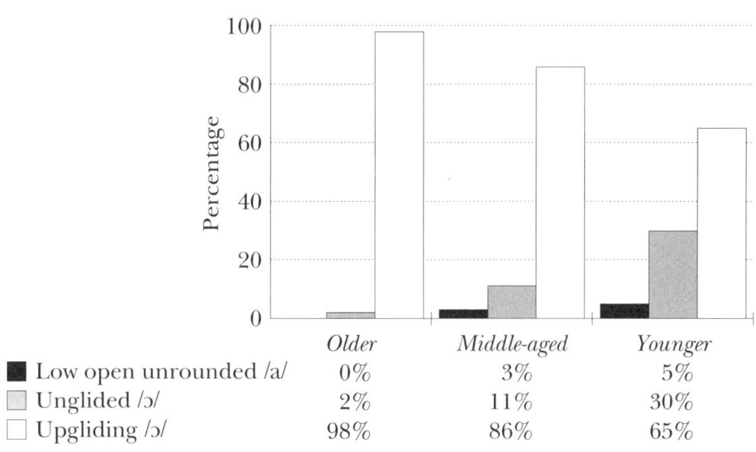


FIGURE 3.13
Decreases in Upgliding /ɔ/, Mill Villagers

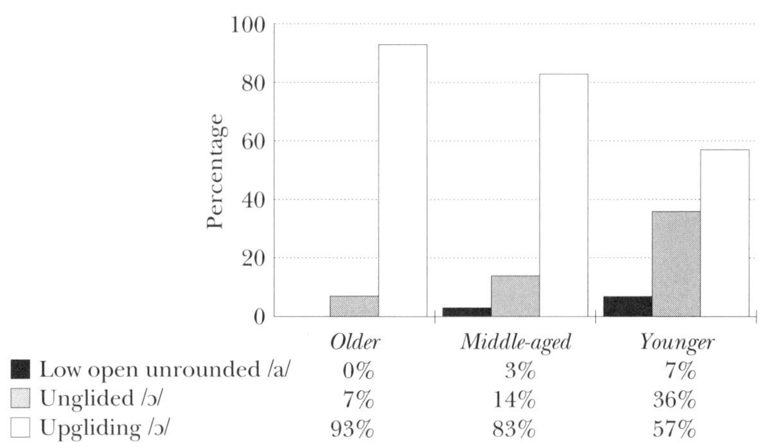


Survey of Texas, and her own surveys of high school students. She finds that the merger is progressing in that area of the South, with attendant sociological constraints of gender (females lead, males rapidly catch up), ethnicity (Anglos and Hispanics participate, but not African Americans), and age (older informants do not have the merger, while high school speakers show 62% merger). The potential influence of Hispanic speakers was considered, but since Spanish has no /ɔ/, these results, in which the merger predominated, were set apart. Tillery also demonstrates that a phonetic hierarchy applies in which the merger occurs most often in environments before voiceless obstruents and least often before voiced velars (–V alveolar > –V labial > –V velar > Ø > nasals > /l/ > +V velar). Unlike Herold's (1990) conclusion of "recategorization," in which phonemic lexical classes trade places (/ɑ/ before /l/ becomes /ɔ/, and vice versa), Tillery finds that the merger in Texas follows Trudgill's (1974) analysis in which two phonemic lexical classes converge (Tillery 1989, 75–76).

Thomas and Bailey (1992) discuss another scenario involving competing mergers, the [ɑ]~[ɔ]~[o] (*far/for/four*) merger. The possible vowel variation introduces several choices for a Southern speaker. For instance, *forty* can be pronounced three different ways: [fɑrɾi], [fɔrɾi], or [forɾi]. Thomas and Bailey found three realizations for these structural possibilities in the set *far*, *for*, and *four*: (1) *for* [fɔːr] can merge with *far* [fɑːr] to become homophones [fɑːr] (the *far/for* merger), (2) *for* [fɔːr] can merge with *four* [foːr] to become homophones [foːr] (the *four/for* merger), or (3) all three classes can remain distinct (180). Their results show that no informants born after World War II maintained the three-way distinction, and the *four/for* merger prevailed over the *far/for* merger. They offer two reasons for the success of the *four/for* merger: (1) the [ɑr] pronunciation is primarily a rural feature, and most of the change in Texas has turned out to be the result of increasing urbanization, and (2) the *far/for* merger was uncommon in areas of spread, such as around Dallas, where features would gain prestige and diffuse outward. They also cite "perhaps a move toward national norms" as an additional motivation (187). The database from Griffin generally confirms this trend of a *four/for* merger, not a surprising result in light of parallel factors of increasing urbanization and proximity to a large city (Atlanta). The only additional detail to note in this instance is the tendency for the lexical item *for* to be pronounced without rhoticization [fə], even in mill speech, or else with extremely marked rhoticization, as in [fɚ]. Its companion lexeme *four* is also often pronounced without rhoticization or with a marked rhoticized variant [foɚ]. Since all of these alternatives are socially marked—dropping of final [r] mirrors African American usage [fo] and emphasis of [r] reflects "Southernness"—their futures as accepted norms seem limited in favor of the less obtrusive form of *for* and *four* as [foɚ] that Bailey has found in Texas.

## CONCLUSION

Through quantitative analysis, the data in Griffin confirms the well-substantiated findings of other researchers concerning the shibboleths of /r/-lessness and /ay/-monophthongization. In the older generations, mill villagers and farmers chose distinctively different options for /r/-pronunciation: the mill villagers, many of whom geographically originated from hill country, overtly pronounced /r/ in all environments, including some insertive instances. On the other hand, farmers dropped their /r/s just as widely. Recent changes for both of these occupational groups has been in the direction of the national norm: farmers have generalized their pronunciation of /r/ over most environments, while mill villagers have "mellowed out" their /r/ pronunciation by eliminating intrusive /r/. A different pattern holds for the variable of /ay/-monophthongization: while generalization of this feature has spread to the most recently affected environment preceding voiceless consonants, the change has not gone to completion and is not even very close. Though the impetus of this change is not quite as vibrant as that of /r/-fullness, a similar tendency of centrism and accommodation can be seen in that mill and farm speakers of middle-aged and younger groups appear to be moving toward a common endpoint.

Speakers from both occupational categories in Griffin do appear to be participating in the chain shifts proposed by Labov, Ash, and Boberg (1997). The overall pattern is one of stable variation with a slight decrease in the younger groups. It is not possible to confirm whether or not this dip is part of continuing stable variation or a reflection of passing changes. While the sound changes of the Southern Shift recorded in this study are perceptible, they are not as phonetically above the level of consciousness as the shibboleths of /r/-deletion and /ay/-monophthongization. Additionally, the exceedingly salient variable of /ay/-monophthongization, which in Labov's configuration encourages and precipitates the entire shift, may play an inhibiting role in the shift as it progresses in Griffin (since /ay/-monophthongization is not progressing in its complete formation).

All speakers in Griffin are participating in the articulatively conducive *pin/pen* merger, but only younger groups show strong signs of the *cot/caught* merger. This latter merger appears to be complicated by the feature of upgliding /ɔ/ recorded by Thomas and Bailey (1992). Younger speakers are moving from upgliding /ɔ/ to unglided /ɔ/, which may be a precursor of the merger with /ɑ/ found by Bailey in Texas or by Labov, Ash, and Boberg (1997).

The most prominent social variations in the Griffin sample occur in the middle-aged groups who grew up in the 1950s era. The general trends of this period coincided with several local changes, including the consolidation of the local high schools at a time when more students were going beyond the seventh grade, the peak of the mill industry (with 13 mills running in 1958), and the widespread collapse of family farms. Bailey (1997) pinpoints this era as a period when many changes took hold that involve southern "norms" today.

The features discussed in this chapter have been identified by relatively recent attestations from linguistic geography, sociolinguistic fieldwork, and some written records. Although many patterns can be described as analogs to patterns in earlier dialects, even as distant as Early Modern English varieties in southern England and Scotch-Irish, all dialects are results of competition and selection. There are many examples of variation in which more than one option is available to any speaker of a certain dialect, with varying constraints on acceptable usage. Each dialect under investigation here is approached as a linguistic construct undergoing constant negotiation by the speakers who use it.

# 4. GRAMMATICAL PATTERNS IN THE LINGUISTIC ECOLOGY OF GRIFFIN, GEORGIA

In this chapter I will profile various syntactic patterns in the Southern White Vernacular English (SWVE) dialects spoken in Griffin. My objectives are to display qualitative findings of local grammatical variables, describe patterns of change over apparent time from a sample that is one hundred years deep, and compare these patterns to trends found in other researchers' work. Factors that influence patterns of change and stability include salience (markedness both phonetically and socially), settlement history, grammaticalization, and social variables (age, gender, community changes).

Table 4.1 shows that the occupational dialects of older speakers generally parallel particular regional dialects; that is, mill-villager speech is similar to Highlands speech, and farmer speech is similar to Lowland speech. As in chapter 3, this first table is modeled after Wolfram, Hazen, and Schilling-Estes's (1999) comparison of features characteristic of subregional dialects. Some features—second-person plural *y'all,* the quasi-modals *gonna* and *fixin to,* and *was/is* generalization in nonstandard verbal concord—are expanding across occupational lines. Other features—perfective *done,* nonstandard verbal *-s* with conjunctive and common NPs—are expanding only in one occupational group. Still other features—*a*-verb-*ing* and double modals—did not show up strongly enough to warrant any projections for maintenance or expansion. The maintenance of nonstandard grammatical features, especially in a population that is increasingly educated, may say a lot about the power of a local "standard" that indexes relationships of identity in the community. Grammatical variation is more sensitive to influence from a "standard" because syntactic features are perceptually salient and indexed to evaluations of education, intelligence, and refinement. The possible influence of both a national prescriptive standard and a local "Southern" standard will be further discussed in the context

TABLE 4.1
Grammatical Comparison of Griffin Features to Characteristic Regional Features

| *Structure* | *Mill Villager* | *Farmer* | *Southern Highland* | *Southern Lowland* | *Non-Southern* |
|---|---|---|---|---|---|
| *a*-verb-*ing* (*He was a-fishin'*) | +/− | +/− | + | +/− | |
| Nonstandard verbs | | | | | |
| Conjuctive NP -*s* concord (*Blinkin and Not gets sleepy*) | + | | + | +/− | |
| Common NP -*s* concord (*The girls climbs the tree*) | + | | + | | |
| *was/is* generalization (*We was there*) | + | +/− | + | + | + |
| Double modals (*He might could come*) | +/− | +/− | +/− | + | |
| Quasi-modals (*fixin to, gonna*) | + | + | + | + | + |
| Second-person plural *y'all* (*y'all come again*) | + | + | + | + | |
| Perfective *done* (*She done messed up*) contrast irregular verb: Generalized particle/past (*She done it*) | + | | + | +/− | |

of recent influxes of non-Southerners and signs of solidarity (chap. 5).

The problem of getting enough tokens to support a grammatically quantitative study is unavoidable in an investigation of this size. Certain features, especially ones that are archaic or fading, are impossible to measure realistically, even with the luxury of the long casual interviews that were pursued in this project. This research is thus qualitative in nature, working with a solid and rigorously compiled database that the researcher knows well. The linguistic structures described here are supplemented by research from linguists who operate in various dialects of the Southeast, including Appalachian English, Ocracoke English, and Ozark English, and those in Texas, east Alabama, and Memphis. These linguists and others have also provided a solid historical foundation for many of the linguistic and sociohistorical progressions that have taken place in the history of American English.

## *A*-VERB-*ING*

In his instructive 1993 study of identifying variables, Wolfram used the well-known and widely reported feature of *a*-verb-*ing*, also known as "*a*-prefixing," to demonstrate how the linguistic context of a variable can become complicated. This apparently simple feature can be restricted by syntactic morphological and phonological parameters:

> *a*- attaches only to those cases of *-ing* which function as a verb or adverb (e.g. *He was running to the store* may attach an *a*-, but *The movie was shocking* may not) and only to forms not headed by a preposition (e.g. *He makes money building houses* may attach an *a*- prefix to *building*, but **He makes money by building houses* may not); there are also phonological restrictions on the potential attachment of the *a*-, as it attaches only to verbs and forms beginning with a consonant (e.g. *fighting* versus **acting*). [Wolfram 1993, 207]

This verbal feature is found in Outer Banks English but is fading now and heard mostly in the speech of older informants and in the telling of animated stories (Wolfram, Hazen, and Schilling-Estes 1999, 46), which suggests that it may be a narrative register. *A*-verb-*ing* is characteristic of isolated areas in the South, and Robert Shackleton's analysis of dialectology records finds it clustered in East Anglia and southwest Devonshire (pers. comm., Jan. 15, 1997). According to Wright's *English Dialect Dictionary* (1898–1905), the combination of *a*-verb-*ing* was "still in common use in Scotland and in the southern Midlands, but not in a broad belt between these two" (Jespersen 1954a, 175). This feature gained usage as part of a "noncommital" designation of verb forms called the "expanded tenses" that came into precise and common usage only in the late seventeenth century (as seen in the styles of John Bunyan and Joseph Addison). Jespersen historicizes the development and decline of *a*-verb-*ing* rather succinctly. The Old English combination of auxiliary verb + participle ending in *-ende* changed to *-inge* and thus became identical to the verbal substantive form. The combination *be on* + substantive differentiated and specified meaning. Later, *on* was replaced by *a-* and then *a-* was dropped by aphesis to result in the frequent and more precise modern usage (Jespersen 1954a, 169). As Wolfram, Hazen, and Schilling-Estes (1999, 46) note, the *a*-construction developed from the attachment of the preposition *at* or *on* as a temporal locative (e.g., *She was at working* 'She was actively engaged in the process of working'). Jespersen (1954a, 179) specifies this expanded tense as a temporal frame that indicates duration of an event as it is relative to other events:

> If we start from the *on -ing* construction: *he is (was) on (= in,* as so often in former times) *hunting* means 'he is (was) in the course of hunting, engaged in hunting, busy (with) hunting'; he is (was) as it were in the middle of something, some protracted action or state, denoted by the substantive *hunting.* The hunting is felt to be a kind of frame around something else; it is represented as lasting some time before and possibly (or probably) also some time after something else, which may or may not be expressly indicated, but which is always in the mind of the speaker. In this way the hunting is thought of as being of *relatively longer duration in comparison with some other fact* (some happening or state, or simply some period or point of time). If we say *he was (on) hunting,* we mean that the hunting had begun, but was not completed at the time mentioned or implied in the sentence, and this element of incompletion (at that time) is very important if we want to understand the expanded tenses, even if it is not equally manifest in all cases. But it should be noted that it is not exactly the period of time that is incomplete, but the action or state indicated by the verb itself.

This characterization of *a*-verb-*ing* clarifies why the form has survived primarily in the discourse of storytelling (though it does perform other semantic functions). The specificity of time reference enables a speaker to recreate the linear progression of events from a past event. In Griffin, it is mostly present in these types of speech acts and more in mill villager speech than in farmer speech. For example, Dolly Prince recalls a young boy she babysat "come up the hill just a-hollerin'" (McKinley 1999). The *a*-construction here pinpoints an event as an action within a larger event to be revealed as the story goes on.

Wolfram and Christian (1976) identified *a*-verb-*ing* in Appalachian English and affirmed its status as an archaism (also Atwood 1953, 42). However, they also noted its decline; in their sample only 3 of 13 speakers under 30 years of age used the form and those instances were at levels less than 20% (74–75). In earlier varieties, the *a*-construction appeared in many dialects in the United States but was most frequent in areas where Appalachian English was spoken by poorly and fairly educated speakers (Atwood 1953, 35; Wolfram and Christian 1976, 69). Atwood found that "very few of the cultured informants" used this construction. This decline is mirrored in Griffin. Only a few instances of this form were recorded:

1. a. You just look at the trees. The trees are part of the world's filter system. A-FILTERING the air you know? [Louis, older mill villager]
   b. And late in the evening Joe would crawl up on this woodpile and preach. You could hear him all over the neighborhood. And I remember Mr. Cy Booker was over there and Joe he was just A-GOING away you know he asked daddy he said What is that? And daddy says Oh that's just Joe preaching. [Flora, older farmer]

## *Y'ALL*

*Y'all* can be described as a unique feature that has no semantic or grammatical counterpart in many other dialects and in standard English, which makes it a prime target of accommodation by outsiders (Montgomery 1996a). The simple conception of the pronoun *y'all* as a second-person plural *you* is probably the most commonly adopted form, but Montgomery posits more diverse functions. He claims that *y'all* "fills a paradigmatic gap, ... functions as an associative plural, [an] institutional plural, [a] potential *y'all* ... plural in one sense but singular in another, [a] collective, [and a] style device" (7–8). These six functions engender misinterpretations and oversimplification, masking the actual demise of a functional category with the apparent spread of the pronoun in the lexicon. Wolfram, Hazen, and Schilling-Estes (1999) record *y'all* in a general sense as a Lowland feature, and they find that it prevails in all of the Outer Banks English varieties; in this way, they find it similar to completive *done* in its spread from Lowland South to isolate varieties that more often align with Highland South features. Bailey et al. (1996) find that *y'all*, along with *might could* and *fixin to*, is expanding in the South. The plural form of *y'all* is common in both varieties in Griffin, but only one instance (2h) was found that could be construed as singular:

2. a. I told her about too I said that's probably what y'all [Rosa's daughter and her friends] saw! You know probably what y'all heard. [Rosa, middle-aged mill villager]
   b. He said I want to come down there and live with you all. [Flora and Roy] Uh live down there close to you said y'all are the only one treat me like anything. [Flora, older farmer]
   c. I think y'all [Flora and J. B.] finally killed him [the snake] didn't you? [Alice, older mill villager]
   d. Next time William comes up, Vivian and I are going to get all y'all [Bob and Edward] together. We're going to make him happy. [Alice, older mill villager]
   e. Bill said why don't y'all [Flora and Roy] just come up so we did. [Flora, older farmer]
   f. She was always "oh I wish y'all [Flora and John] would get married wah wah wah." And if she'd have kept her mouth shut we'd have got along lots better. [Flora, older farmer]
   g. Oh yeah. Dundee Mills, you know what I'm talking about? So y'all [Lisa and Maureen] must be from down that way. [William, middle-aged farmer]
   h. I'm gonna take y'all [Randall] back to where I found you. [Louis, older mill villager]

## MULTIPLE MODALS

Like *y'all*, the construction of multiple modals (attributed usually to Lowland South) is a complex syntactic pattern that does not have a semantic or grammatical counterpart in other dialects. Unlike *y'all*, the complexity of multiple modals is apparent enough to discourage adoption by outsiders. Montgomery (1996a, 12), in fact, claims that, in comparing possible combinations of modal forms, we begin to see the structural nature of multiple modals as not a typical grammatical feature or set of forms, but as exponents of a linguistic subsystem that permits certain modalities to be combined. Linguistically speaking, it is the ability of speakers to combine modals, not merely to know one or more given combinations, that distinguishes these speakers from others.

From Montgomery's statement we might hypothesize that a sociolinguistic value accompanies performance in the use of this feature; however, he reports that *y'all* has more social prestige than multiple modals, and others find no evidence of social valuation (Feagin 1979, 151–75; Di Paolo 1986; Butters 1991; Mishoe and Montgomery 1994) except that some forms appear more often in recorded African American speech (*Linguistics Atlas of the Gulf States,* as reported in Mishoe and Montgomery 1994). Butters, who studied multiple modals collected by elicitation, also noted that African Americans and whites differed in the use of modal forms, especially combined with negation, and tentatively suggested that such instances of "*must/might* + *do* + neg. could be viewed as an early instance of linguistic divergence of [Black English Vernacular] in New York City" (1991, 173).

The pragmatics additionally involve face-to-face interactions that often involve negotiation or hedging and are thus not easily recorded in interviews (14). Nevertheless, Bailey (1997, 269–70) verifies that multiple modals are a later change that probably picked up speed after the Civil War (judging from evidence from ex-Confederates in Brazil) and expanded into general usage by 1930. It is not clear how the spread of this feature correlates to its semantic and grammatical complexity. In Griffin, I have heard farmers use multiple modals with more frequency than mill villagers. In line with Montgomery, multiple modals usually occur in contexts of negotiation. For example, one exchange in which I was trying to make another contact went like this:

3. INTERVIEWER: Maybe you could hook me up with her too.
   FLORA: She MIGHT COULD. She was a funny little gal.

In this instance, the double modals "reinforce the idea of mitigation or tentativeness, possibility rather than definite probability"

(Ching 1987, 337). Atwood (1953, 35) isolates the phrase *might could* as a future marker commonly used by South and South Midland speakers of poor and fair education (and also in the German area of Pennsylvania). He finds that "cultured" informants avoid the construction, but that it is very common in fairly educated speakers. He also connects the form *mought* (not found in the Griffin sample) with double modals. Atwood shows broad coverage of *might could* that reaches into the German area of Pennsylvania and is present in much of the area of the Appalachian Mountains (42). In Griffin, very few instances were found. The speech in (3) and (4) indicate lack of determination.

4. a. I was a mere baby so I don't have a clue. I MIGHT WOULDA been one or two years old I don't know. [William, middle-aged farmer]
   b. I said I know we MIGHT OUGHTA take her to the doctor but Granny said Let's go to the drugstore so I did. And he gave her something. [Alice]

## QUASI-MODALS

The cognomen of this syntactic item suggests that it is perhaps a category in flux. Indeed, much of the current discussion of *fixin to* and *gonna* is gravitating to the process of grammaticalization. Following Harris (1997), who is following Meillet (1912), I am using the narrow definition of grammaticalization: "Meillet's sense of grammaticalization includes the process by which a word becomes a clitic, a clitic an affix, and an affix a synchronically unanalyzable part of another morpheme; it includes the processes of phonological reduction and semantic bleaching which often accompany the processes named above" (Harris 1997). The term QUASI-MODAL is almost ironic in that it would seem to mean 'almost, but not quite' (*quasi*) that which is 'almost a verb but used primarily to indicate mood' (*modal*). As Lyons (1968) notes, modals are often slippery customers in all languages. In English, they sometimes function as past-tense forms but sometimes do not. When they do not have reference to past time, "the 'tense' distinction of non-past *v.* past would seem to subcategorize the modality in question in such a way that 'past' combines with mood to introduce a more 'tentative', 'remote' or 'polite' sense. In other words, 'tense' is here 'converted' into a secondary modality" (311). The following discussion attempts to deal with this inherent changeability in two forms that are rapidly expanding in Southern dialects, *fixin to* and *gonna.*

The quasi-modal *fixin to* is spreading throughout the South in a "contagious rather than hierarchical" pattern, according to Bailey et al. (1993). Formerly a rural phenomenon, *fixin to* is spreading from rural areas to urban areas even as other Southern features are receding. Two explanations are offered for this "mirror image" of recession and expansion. First, *fixin to* has spread with urbanization much like the scattered, low-frequency phonological variation of /ɛ/ and /ɪ/ before nasals in Tennessee (377) and, second, the expansion of this traditional Southern feature may be a way of affirming local identity in cities inundated by "outsiders" from other regions of the country (378). Like *y'all, fixin to* seems to be unmarked with regard to level of education and easily applicable to a range of common usages. Also, *fixin to* may be grouped with Montgomery's assessment of *y'all* and double modals as having no equivalent in other dialects. Ching (1987) identifies three "core concepts" for the semantic content of *fixin to*: the quasi-modal signifies a sense of immediacy after a short delay, a commissive intent, and a durative meaning of preparation (+punctual infinitive). If any of these core concepts is violated, then native speakers deem the usage either unacceptable or ironic. Following Ching, Aucoin (1997) characterizes *fixin to* not as a marker of futurity but rather "as denoting immediate action after a short delay," as in "getting ready to do something."

In the data from Griffin, there are at least two categories of immediacy that can easily be distinguished. First, *fixin to* can denote a point in time when an event commences, or should commence.

5. a. And I remember mama was FIXIN TO take Mary out to the bus station. And everybody down there was looking for that dress. And Snoot and I were sitting up there in the door to the loft. [Flora, older farmer]
   b. Well mostly girls lived in there the apartments, and I had the top apartment on that side and the way I got it I moved in with some other girls and they pitched a party one night after me

and Evelyn went to work. and Mr Irving was FIXING TO come in and had wait just—to throw us out. I said "well you wait just a minute buster I wasn't there!" He finally let me have the apartment. [Flora, older farmer]

Other uses do indicate a short or moderate delay:

6. a. He's FIXING TO go in the seminary. [Bob, older farmer]
   b. And uh so here they find Mr. Young finally brought him back AND IT'S TIME I WAS FIXING TO GO HOME. Nathan said I'll take you Mr. Young said are you crazy? "No." So we got out and he said "Let's go get something to eat!" [Flora, older farmer]

Bailey (1997) has remarked on the spread of *fixin to* in terms of linguistic evolution; although it was attested in 1829, it probably became frequent in the last quarter of the nineteenth century; thus it emerged later than the colonial period and cannot be easily traced to British varieties. Bailey and Tillery (1996) and Aucoin (1997) assert that

> *Fixin to* is the result of a grammaticalization process which blends *to fix to* and *to fix for* (as in 'They fixed for going to the parsonage early the next morning') into a new auxiliary form [perhaps in the direction of *fixin to* → *finna* → *fin*]. [Aucoin 1997, 2]

In the same way, *gonna, gon,* and *go* instantiate the grammaticalization of *going to.* Atwood describes this process as "phonetic reduction" (1953, 37). This latter form is much more common in speech in all varieties in Griffin and, I suspect, varieties throughout the United States. At any rate, both forms were easy to find in both of the targeted speech communities.

The phrase *going to* is similar to *fixin to* in several ways. Both forms have lost their original semantic content as verbs and have become

> empty, grammatical word[s].... The weakening of the original meaning is particularly clear when it becomes possible to say 'I am going to go'. [Jespersen 1954a, 217]

Parallel to this weaker construction of *going to* might be the grammatically acceptable *I am fixin to fix (that lamp).* Both forms also mark futurity, often with a sense of immediacy. However, *going to* does not require as strictly a constrained sense of immediacy as *fixin to* does for acceptability: (1) *not to the child you are now, but to the man you are going to be*; (2) **not to the child you are now, but to the man you are fixin to be.* Furthermore, there is a register difference here: *going to* is informal but "standard" while *fixing to* is not "standard" (Ronald R. Butters, pers. comm., Aug. 22, 2005).

Another commonality between the two forms is use as a signifier of intent or commitment (Jespersen 1954a; Ching 1987). This function warrants the label "prospective" (Jespersen 1954a, 218). The construction *going to* is first seen in the late fifteenth century but does not become common until after 1600. Jespersen also traces the synonym *getting to*—as in *I'm getting to be an old man*—back to 1912, and he characterizes this combination as "rare."

Both *gonna* and *fixin* are evident throughout the speech of all speakers in Griffin. An early stage of the grammaticalization process (similar to the early form *to fix to*) is illustrated in Patty's description of how her father injured his abdomen:

7. It was high steps and he was putting up some new steps. All steps back then were wood. They were very steep and it was some children playing out in the yard. And he had asked the mother to get the children and take em in because they could get injured. And she didn't do it. It was a child ran under the steps JUST AS HE WAS FIXED TO hang em and he pulled a-back and just ruined his abdomen to keep from squashing a child. And uh they uh took him to the hospital of course and back then they couldn't repair stuff like that like they can now. He always had trouble wi—and they had to work him and give him whatever he could do till he died. [Patty, older mill villager]

Patty's usage still retains explicit tense markers, including the copula *was* and the affix *-ed* instead of the continuous progressive form *-ing*. A more advanced stage of the grammaticalization process show up in Larry's telling of a joke:

8. but uh it's like the old joke about the guy that won a big pile of money and they asked him what he was GON do with it, and he says I'm ONNA farm till it's all gone. [Larry, middle-aged mill villager]

In the first instance, the form *gon* has lost both tense affix and *to*. In the second instance, *onna* is practically an affix to *I'm* [a::mɔnə]. Semantic categories can also be distinguished for *gonna*. In the Griffin sample, there are instances where *gonna* indicates something that was planned but never was and never will be executed:

9. a. He was GONNA be a professional ball player and all of a sudden he decided to be a minister. [Zelda, older mill villager]
   b. I thought he was GONNA quit eating. He almost quit eating. But he called the waitress over there and told her about it and showed it to her and they come apologizing you know I mean that happens. [Rosa, middle-aged mill villager]
   c. well see uh we had a calf one time. Daddy got a calf, was GONNA raise it. [Rosa, middle-aged mill villager]
   d. He invited me to come up there one Sunday and we was GONNA kill some chickens and get em ready to go in the freezer and uh he couldn't ring their necks [Rosa, middle-aged mill villager]
   e. WE WAS GONNA GO to Wal-Mart and it rained so hard that the car was drownding out on us. [Rosa, middle-aged mill villager]
   f. But that's how all mine happened, it's just uh—she asked for it uh—I was GONNA call it Living Memories. [Rosa, middle-aged mill villager]

It is also possible to use *gonna* to indicate plans that may or may not be completed at some point in the future:

10. a. . . . like every five minutes. Like he did when I got out. We went to jail the same day and I got out before he did, he called me like, ever since I got out until he got out. Like every five ten minutes, are you GONNA come get me? are you GONNA come get me? [Deena, younger mill villager]
    b. And working online and uh, matter of fact I'm GONNA get in there and try to get started on the last two chapters. [Rosa, middle-aged mill villager]
    c. But I talk about the people that I worked with and I'm GONNA see if I can get them to come sit down and talk to me bring me a picture of em to put in the book. [Rosa, middle-aged mill villager]
    d. I'm hoping that one day'll come when I can quit smoking. I'm not GONNA give up on it. [Rosa, middle-aged mill villager]

Finally, a third category denotes serious intent, perhaps even a directive, issued with finality:

11. a. And it's never GONNA be like that again. [Rosa, middle-aged mill villager]
    b. But still daddy's have to get out there and ring their necks. And momma—oh yeah I'm GONNA tell you what. He had he was raising chickens for a while and had a lot of em. [Rosa, middle-aged mill villager]
    c. Cause you kinda want to give em enough information to make em want to read it but not enough to uh tell em all that GONNA happen. [Rosa, middle-aged mill villager]
    d. And one of his daughters became a lawyer and she had to defend somebody that was guilty and she just quit. She said naw I'm not GONNA do that. I'm not GONNA get this guy off or no guy off. And she done gone to school and everything else to become a lawyer. [Louis, older mill villager]
    e. But uh the next book IS GONNA BE DONE for my cousin and his company. [Rosa, middle-aged mill villager]
    f. we ain't GONNA have no deep dark secrets. [Zelda, older mill villager]
    g. yeah hopefully it's just that cause if they send me back for a year or two I'm I'm GONNA go crazy I don't want to go back to jail for awhile. [Steve, younger mill villager]
    h. uh, the people saw no reason for a union and uh .. and earlier when they still had the the trust relationship .. uh, they were not interested because they felt like hey my company's GONNA take care of me I don't need this. [Gerald, middle-aged mill villager]
    i. But really her outlook on the mill people were that they were mill people and they weren't they weren't ever GONNA be anything but mill people. [Louis, older mill villager]
    j. May as well tell me cause I'm GONNA hire somebody to find out. [Louis, older mill villager]
    k. I says I'm GONNA take you and you GONNA tell your wife what's going on here. Got to started down through there and I said Billy how many kids you got? He says four. I thought for a minute I says nah I turned around he says what you doing? I'm GONNA take yall back to where I found you. I says I'm not GONNA tell your wife I say I don't want to tear the heart out of her. If you wanna do that you can. I said but if I ever catch yall

together again I'm GONNA whoop both of you. [Louis, older mill villager]

l. I was bound and determined that I was GONNA get a job in Griffin. [Larry, middle-aged mill villager]

m. well I'm GONNA pull around so I can understand you. [William, middle-aged farmer]

One interesting observation is the occurrence of *gonna* unaccompanied by verb tense elsewhere in the sentence:

12. a. yeah. what Ø you GONNA do though. I mean you got to. [William, middle-aged farmer]

b. so you don't know what they Ø gonna do [William, middle-aged farmer]

c. you Ø GONNA knock the ashtray over again [Annie, middle-aged mill villager]

These forms *are* carrying implied tense while indicating modality. Lyons's (1968, 309–11) analysis seems applicable in these instances in that tense intersects with mood. The potential in these forms is a verb construction that functions as a mood marker and intersects variably with tense. Semantic bleaching and phonological reduction are contributing to a process that may result in two further grammaticized forms, *gon* and *fin*, that are not, as Harris (1997) and Meillet (1912) would predict, "synchronically analyzable." As for the spread of both *gonna* and *fixin*, the innocuous nature of these quasi-modals along with phonetically effortless grammaticalization would seem to ensure their success not only in Southern dialects but also perhaps in a spread beyond regional boundaries.

## NONSTANDARD VERB PATTERNS

Many subject-verb concord patterns distinguish Southern dialects both from each other and from other regions. The prescriptive standard subject-verb agreement is but one factor in a plethora of options. Appalachian English and Ozark English, for example, are similar to each other and different from African American Vernacular English in subject-verb concord deviations from standard

American English (Hazen 1996; citing Christian, Wolfram, and Dube 1988, 27). While the paradigms from southern England show up in all Southern American varieties, a nonstandard concord pattern of inflectional *-s* in Appalachian English, Ocracoke English, and Ozark English is sourced to Scots and Ulster dialects that overwhelmingly favor verbal *-s* and *has/was* in all environments except when the subject is pronominal and adjacent to the verb. Due to migration routes and settlement patterns, speakers selected verbal patterns from multiple options of subject-verb concord in British dialects, with currently standard American subject-verb concord having evolved more from dialects in southern England. Montgomery (1994a, 89) found that in Scots, due to the conjunction of the "Type of Subject Constraint" and the "Proximity to Subject Constraint," inflectional *-s* was added to essentially all verbs "unless the subject NP was an adjacent personal pronoun" (Hazen 1996, 28). Thus, the rate of inflectional *-s* was very high in Scots. Inflectional *-s* may have expanded in Northumbrian and Scots to third-person plural, and then consolidated through some leveling during the Middle and Early Modern English period, but "similar syntactic categories that trigger nonstandard concord and a similar ordering of the variable constraints on nonstandard concord" are the common threads that Hazen uses to link Scotch and Irish English to modern-day isolate varieties (50). This pattern, in Hazen's description, extends to the postinsular American varieties. Montgomery (1996b, 233) identifies variation in his study of verbal *-s* and counters the assumption that southern Englishes are simple koinézations: "dialect diversity, especially reflected in style shifting, was the rule." Atwood (1953, 41–42) deems *you was* versus *you were* as the closest thing to a shibboleth in the South and mentions Early Modern English origins.

In the Griffin data, nonstandard verbal patterns that match with Hazen's findings show up prolifically in the mill speakers of all ages and in both males and females:

13. Conjunctive NPs
    a. we lived on the village and we were... ME AND HIS SISTER WAS good, well BOTH HIS SISTERS WAS good friends. [Zelda, older mill villager]

b. The warp. You put a new warp on the—see THE TOWELS AND ALL IS MADE of yarn on a big beam. [Alfred, older mill villager]
c. Well it wasn't paved when MAMA AND DADDY WAS there. [Alice]
D. YOUR PAPA AND FLORA'S MAMA WAS brother and sister. [Alice]
e. I mean my brother, ME AND MY BROTHER WAS—WE WAS the way we grew up, see my brother's my stepbrother. [Steve, younger mill villager]

14. Plural NPs
    a. I just don't think they done enough for THE BOYS THAT WAS in service. Myself. That's the way I feel. I don't know whether OTHER PEOPLE FEELS that way or not. [Zelda, older mill villager]
    b. ALL OF MY GENERATIONS HAS BEEN HERE. And all of my children lives within about six or seven miles of me. So uh, I say not many people got that MANY CHILDREN THAT LIVES that close by. [Zelda, older mill villager]
    c. They used to that just like PEOPLE THAT'S FARMERS IS USED TO PLOWING in the heat. [Alfred, older mill villager]
    d. THE CARDS MAKES what they call drawing. [Alfred, older mill villager]
    e. They got THESE SPOOLS THAT MAKES it one color, white, it's striped see? [Alfred, older mill villager]
    f. naw, you can't—all them houses down there—ALL THEM HOUSES DOWN THERE WAS A VILLAGE. [Alfred, older mill villager]
    g. Well she—they come home scared to death one day. Said that wood—THEM WOODS IS HAUNTED. [Rosa, middle-aged mill villager]
    h. THESE NEW ONES HAS got the computers and all on em. [Rosa, middle-aged mill villager]
    i. and we all worked together you know and MOST OF EM WAS on the second shift. [Rosa, middle-aged mill villager]
    j. and every, like my house on THREE SIDES WAS cornfields and on the front was the road, so… [Kelly, younger mill villager]
15. Personal Pronouns
    a. I taught mine when THEY WAS little coming up how to clean and cook and everything. [Zelda, older mill villager]

b. But they when we moved over here THEY WAS. [Alfred, older mill villager]
c. You remember ... YOU WAS done living over there when they cut Northside Drive through. [Alfred, older mill villager]
d. What IS YOU trying to do Miss Alice? [Alfred, older mill villager]
e. Now, talk about the cotton mills, now they're more modern now than THEY WAS back then. [Alfred, older mill villager]
f. we started beating him and we told him if we saw that he went to sleep that WE WAS going to take him and kill him [Steve, younger mill villager]
g. My grandma raised us. She did a real good job on it but we just didn't listen. The way WE WAS RAISED with my stepmamma and we got put with my grandmamma. [Steve, younger mill villager]
h. And they finally in 1888 it come together. And THEY WAS able to put em up, uh John Cheatham they moved him in here. [Rosa, middle-aged mill villager]
i. It's all we ever knowed. You know that's the only thing we ever knew. And uh, it felt close because we knew everybody and in a way it was like WE WAS all family. [Rosa, middle-aged mill villager]
j. One day WE WAS there waiting and one of daddy's coworkers come out—we called her Aunt Mae— [Rosa, middle-aged mill villager]
k. He said I can't hire you until YOU's eighteen. [Rosa, middle-aged mill villager]
l. I mean it's just abandoned houses or HOUSES THAT's not taken care of and uh rental property... [Rosa, middle-aged mill villager]
m. THEM'S UGLY ANIMALS [Rosa, middle-aged mill villager]
n. Well see we uh when WE WAS growing up about the only meat we had was chicken. [Rosa, middle-aged mill villager]

In the farm sample, no nonstandard constructions were found using conjunctive NPs. A few instances of common NPs showed up in mostly convoluted phrases, and the majority of nonstandard verb patterns were found in one older female speaker, Flora, with personal pronouns in subject position:

16. Plural NPs
    a. There was a—I guess in a way there probably was a little bit of a class system. In this county you had city kids THAT WAS THE ONES that went to Griffin High [Bob, older farmer]
    b. COURSE THERE WAS SOME PEOPLE THAT UH THERE WERE SOME PEOPLE that were black marketeers and bootleggers and that sort of thing where for a price maybe you find something you know. [Bob, older farmer]
    c. I mean that was the job to have in Griffin. When THE MILLS WAS KICKING before the foreigners took it over. you know. overseas, started selling stuff real cheap. [William, middle-aged farmer]
17. Personal Pronouns
    a. WE WASN'T. but uh but he and I had more fun just doing crazy things. I remember he used to come down at the house and he wouldn't much more than get there than Aunt Flora would send Joe after him. so when he got there we'd start and get us a piece of paper and draw what WE WAS GOING TO DO when Joe came after him. [Flora, older farmer]
    b. and WE WAS AT HOME and it was during—before–just a while before Christmas and he went back he went to work at the post office I said what you doing licking stamps? [Flora, older farmer]
    c. and WE WAS SITTING THERE EATING and I looked up and there was snakeskin it must have been it was opened up about that wide and about oh uh, I didn't go there no more. [Flora, older farmer]
    d. and THEY WAS WORKING on these airplanes and I sat out on the end of the wing and these little old boys out there. [Flora, older farmer]
    e. It's just beautiful. But we had ... WE WAS unfortunate ... we only spent one night and two days and it rained the whole time. [Edward, older farmer]

A very interesting finding is that other nonstandard verb patterns, such as Ø copula, durative *been*, and nonstandard singular subject + plural verb concord, were found in a number of speakers in the farm sample but none were found in the mill sample. The same speaker who crosses over in the personal pronoun subject-verb concord pattern, Flora, also has adopted nonstandard subject-verb patterns that reflect a completely different dialect group (AAVE). Also included in this list is the occurrence of durative *been* in older white farm speakers.

18. Ø Copula
    a. I think Charlie died not too long ago but RUBY Ø STILL THERE. [Flora, older farmer]
    b. . . . THEY Ø BOTH DEAD NOW. [Flora, older farmer]
    c. he wasn't—that's the first colored person I'VE EVER KNOW(N) that wasn't afraid of snakes as long as he could see them. [Flora, older farmer]
    d. I said WHAT Ø YOU DOING LICKING STAMPS? [Flora, older farmer]
    e. So we were flipping for nickels I mean, you know, that's all you did, something like that, THEY DIDN'T NOBODY WORK. [Flora, older farmer]
    f. Snoot. That's what he was always called till suddenly Granny DECIDE he was Edward. [Flora, older farmer]
19. Nonstandard Singular Subject + Plural Verb Concord
    a. We lived within what's the city limits of Griffin now and THERE WERE NO ELECTRICITY until I was fifteen years old. [Bob, older farmer]
    b. But really HER OUTLOOK ON THE MILL PEOPLE WERE that they were mill people and they weren't they weren't ever gonna be anything but mill people. [Louise, middle-aged farmer]
20. *been*
    a. I Ø BEEN WORKING DOWN I BEEN Ø WORKING on the flight line ever since there was a flight line and I want to go back. [Flora, older farmer]
    b. ... and he bought that and HE Ø BEEN THERE ABOUT NOT QUITE A YEAR AND WE JUST STARTED TO MOVE IN ON IT. [Flora, older farmer]
    c. I can remember a kid in the next desk said uh I KNOW WHERE YOU Ø BEEN this morning... in the cow barn! [Bob, older farmer]
    d. people I BEEN KNOWING forty years I can't call their names sometimes! [Edward, older farmer]

## PERFECTIVE AND COMPLETIVE *DONE*

Wolfram and Christian (1976) characterized perfective *done* as completive *done* because it has developed so that it does not replace perfect tense. In their study of Appalachian English, it is found in constructions with past verb tenses or intervening between an auxiliary and a main verb without changing form itself. Thus, they agree with Labov, Yaeger, and Steiner (1972, 56) that since it does not change tenses, it has "lost its status as a verb." In their samples, *done* functions as a modifier of other past tense verbal constructions, as an additional aspect marker for past actions or events, and, since it does not work with a progressive or with continuity adverbs (e.g., *often*), they find that "the distinctiveness of *done* ... appears to lie instead in its 'completive' aspect" (87). Stylistically, completive *done* is used for emphasis to indicate that something has definitely happened. They add that it is a stigmatized form in Appalachian English and most tokens occurred in the speech of older males. Though it is a form that they claim is likely dying out, they also left room for the possibility that it just did not occur naturally in interviews.

In a different scenario, Feagin (1986a) finds that perfective *done* is stable and used more by women and girls than by men and boys. Its sameness across rural and urban samples shows acknowledgment of two separate norms, and "adherence to solidarity norms [versus prestige norms] enforced by networks" (226). Feagin adds that this feature is implicated in debates over the relationship of AAVE and SWVE. Creolists, like Dillard (1972) and Stewart (1967), claim that perfective *done* was originally a deep structure AAVE feature that has been imitated by whites. Variationists, on the other hand, claim that examples such as perfective *done* only evidence "low-level rules which have marked effects on surface structure" (Labov et al. 1968). Its use in Gullah is of intensification and aspect, where it is recorded with uninflected verbs such as *eat*: "I done eat" (Mille 1997, 108–10). In their research, Wolfram and Christian (1976) noted that Traugott (1972) has documented that it used to occur with the present tense, and Atwood has found that this is still true in AAVE. Perhaps this is part of the reason for the stigmatization of the form that Wolfram and Christian noted in Appalachian English.

In the Griffin sample, perfective and completive *done* are evident across age and gender lines in the mill speaker sample while only one farm speaker uses these forms. In every instance, this particular farm speaker, an older female, uses emphatic *done* in the phrase *I done forgot*:

21. a. We carried him down and looked at some apartments . . . little old tacky one bedroom apartment that was about—I DONE FORGOT—six seven hundred dollars a month you know. [Flora, older farmer]
    b. yeah but the main place where I ever went was when I was working. We used to go to someplace where you'd dance—I DONE FORGOT—great big place and it had a big ol' light in the middle. [Flora, older farmer]

This same fixed usage also shows up in mill speakers, as with an older male:

22. I stopped through there going somewhere I DONE FORGOT. Ohio I guess. [Louis, older mill villager]

Various uses of *done* appear in male, female, young, middle-aged, and older speakers in the mill sample. As expected, this form shows up accompanied by a past form of the verb and between an auxiliary and main verb:

23. a. well I DONE run off at the mouth enough you can turn that thing off [Louis, older mill villager]
    b. We didn't know what a hamburger was. Till we DONE got grown, you know. [Rosa, middle-aged mill villager]
    c. yes off and on. He was an accountant. He had DONE worked a lot of different jobs during his life but uh he spent a good many years keeping books. [Gerald, middle-aged mill villager]
    d. I believe I've—I believe I've DONE forgot how to do it. [Alfred, older mill villager]
    e. no that's what we was told okay and this is a good story in itself. In August of eighteen—eighteen, ninety eighty two, my

daddy had DONE got to where he couldn't hardly work. He'd just given out. Same thing I do today. I just walk a little bit and give out. So he went to a doctor they done a complete physical on him. [Rosa, middle-aged mill villager]

It also serves as an additional aspect marker of past completion and for emphasis:

24. a. Well you ain't gonna believe what happened to us Saturday night. My husband loves to go to the lighthouse. Every Saturday night. I've DONE got tired of it. But we were sitting there and talking and he's stirring up his slaw and found a fly. [Rosa, middle-aged mill villager]
    b. And one of his daughters became a lawyer and she had to defend somebody that was guilty and she just quit. She said naw I'm not gonna do that. I'm not gonna get this guy off or no guy off. And she DONE gone to school and everything else to become a lawyer. [Louis, older mill villager]
    c. well see they DONE sold all this out now to individuals. [Zelda, older mill villager]

Also, perfective *done* is used with both an auxiliary and a past participle to indicate a complex verbal construction in which the speaker references a state in the past when an event had not yet occurred.

25. I went up there on Sunday morning I hadn't DONE seen her. And she had long black, she rolled her hair up then, and always wore a great big flower right up there. She had a white one. First time we seen her though it was a red rose. [Alfred, older mill villager]

However, Griffin speakers use *done* as an irregular main verb for *did* without an auxiliary, though *done* does not ever change form.

26. a. You know what he DONE to me? [Deena, younger mill villager]
    b. He DONE that every night at our house. He'd come out there on that front porch and he'd stick them two fingers in his mouth and whistle. Us young'uns knew we better head on home. He DONE that in the summertime about ten o'clock, but in the winter, it was eight. [John, middle-aged farmer]

c. Ed stopped what he was doing and DONE whatever it was the man wanted done and as he left he told your dad to put it on his book. [John, middle-aged farmer]

d. That's the way most people DONE. Got things way back they gave it away or throw it away, that they just hang on to it be worth some money. [Alfred, older mill villager]

e. I mean I just went from one to the other and I DONE like you're doing. [Rosa, middle-aged mill villager]

f. See that's what we DONE for so many years. Because up until that mill shut down I didn't know what it was like to have to drive to work. [Rosa, middle-aged mill villager]

g. so they had to start putting houses. They didn't do it to make money they DONE it to get the workers you know so they could keep their workers and that's how it all started and it happened around every mill that started up. [Rosa, middle-aged mill villager]

In other instances, *done* substitutes for AUX + *do*.

27. a. course I've enjoyed what I DONE most of those years anyway. [Bob, older farmer]

b. We couldn't none of us pass the breathing test. You know cause we DONE so much. When I went to work for Dundee I couldn't pass it. [Rosa, middle-aged mill villager]

c. Well she come out of hers and she DONE real good. But she wadn't never able to you know hold down a job again cause she had done got older and then she just stayed at home. [Zelda, older mill villager]

In the following instances, *done* even takes an object:

29. a. they said it was accidental but a lot of the people on the mill village didn't think it was accidental they thought it was his son DONE it. [Rosa, middle-aged mill villager]

b. And they was able to put em up, uh John Cheatham they moved him in here from South Carolina and he DONE the management and it just went from there. [Rosa, middle-aged mill villager]

c. and right now it's hard because my grandfather, my step-grandfather he just got put in the hospital because something happened a while back he fell, when he got in the car accident he started bleeding like in his brain and they DONE a CAT scan and they just now found it so he's up there at Emory with his granddaughter his granddaughter works up there and he just got out of surgery today so they're up there now checking on him seeing how he's doing and everything. [Deena, younger mill villager]

d. And uh she run a sewing machine hem end towels. And he DONE a lot of jobs. [Paul, older mill villager]

e. He graduated in May, he married in May, and he left here about two weeks after they got back off their honeymoon and went on uh first of June up there. So he DONE a hard year's work. [Zelda, older mill villager]

There is also one occurrence where the speaker uses *done* with a progressive to indicate a state of continuity that existed in the past:

29. you remember when all of that was pasture down there. You was DONE living over there when they cut Northside Drive through. ['You were living over there when they cut Northside Drive through'; Alfred, older mill villager]

Finally, an example of *done* meaning 'finish' shows that the grammaticalization process is progressing semantically:

30. He went to college and graduated, DONE his college in three years and now he's in a church. [Zelda, older mill villager]

Judging from the data from mill workers in Griffin, *done* is still in use as (an irregular) past-tense verb. It replaces past tense for speakers across age and gender boundaries, pairs with progressives, and is able to take an object. Stylistically, the mill speakers reflect Feagin's observation that perfective *done* is a solidarity marker; the form is certainly not stigmatized enough to curb usage in any age group. The productive mill pattern does not, however, provide support in relation to any implication with AAVE dialects. Mill villages, while no longer segregated, still do not sustain intimate contact between African Americans and whites, and historically the mill villagers have lived in more segregated conditions than farmers (who show rare instances of perfective *done*).

## CONCLUSION

Although occupational and regional patterns can be correlated in older speakers, time of emergence does not necessarily coordinate with regional distributional patterns. For example, multiple modals in Lowland speech probably did not enter into general usage until after 1870, whereas both *y'all* and *fixin to* are probably slightly earlier developments, being first attested in 1824 and 1829, respectively, then becoming common toward the end of the nineteenth century (Bailey 1997, 268). Furthermore, these three features are not clearly traceable to British or Scotch-Irish dialects. On the other hand, subject-verb concord patterns of verbal *-s* in Highland speech can convincingly be linked to Scotch-Irish origins, compounded by the isolation of speakers who maintained this feature in their dialects (Appalachian English, Ocracoke English, and Ozark English). These verbal patterns were well established by 1870 but have declined ever since, except in isolated pockets and tight-knit communities.

Since some nonstandard features are spreading while others are not, the factor of being nonstandard or indicative of a solidarity measure is not in itself a sole motivator for change in either direction. Options of subject-verb concord, for instance, are at crux where either nonstandard forms are phasing out (nonstandard verbal *-s* is not found in farm speech, even that of hyperdialectal Flora) or spreading from mill to farm (as in the case of *was/is* generalization). At the same time, perceptual categories of education/intelligence/refinement versus Southernness are competing. Rosa exemplifies the lifestyle and dialectal choices of one committed to a community norm but attempts at correction are found in other speakers. Still, farm speakers joining the trend imply that Atwood's designation of *you was* as a shibboleth may be true, or at least may have been true in the past, as seen in Flora's vigorous usage. Innovated forms, such as *y'all, gonna,* and *fixin to,* are spreading not only across dialects but also across regional lines. On the other hand, it is difficult to determine the status of the items *a*-verb-*ing* and double modals. Instances of these items are rare in current data in the literature and only three instances were recorded on tape from interviews in Griffin. There is not enough evidence to assert that these features are dying out, and regarding multiple modals, Mishoe and Montgomery (1994) make a convincing case that there is not even enough evidence to conclude that multiple modals are not older forms.

So, the answer as to why one option is chosen over another remains a puzzle informed by various features in an ecological mix. Here we have seen the influence of settlement patterns, salience, and indexical significance, as well as phonetic simplicity, semantic bleaching, and grammaticalization. What were the dominant traits of the founder population in the mill villages? This question will be explored in the next chapter, which examines not only community norms and prescriptive standards, but also the speaker networks that fix general patterns of dialectal evolution.

# 5. SOCIAL NETWORKS AND LINGUISTIC EVOLUTION: A BRIEF CASE STUDY

The dialects of Griffin are the result of population shifts and ensuing contact equations. Griffin is a town that was segregated and separated in the first decades of the twentieth century, paving the way for at least two separate varieties. The initial discrete evolutions of each dialect occurred because of different structural and ethnographic factors. Separate socioeconomic histories—including different places of dialect origin, different cultural backgrounds, and different occupational status—ensured different kinds of contact between settlers first in America and then in local communities. The original settlers of the Griffin agricultural region established farms in the new territory and traced their roots to earlier American settlers who had come from various parts of England, including many from southern England. Mill workers came later and became the founder population of the mill villages. Their ancestors were later arrivals to America who came from the Borderlands of north England, Ireland, and Scotland and settled in the hill country of the southern Appalachians. As individual speakers negotiated the socioeconomic shifts that occurred in the twentieth century, the two speech communities engaged in more contact with each other, and yet another phase of dialect evolution took place in Griffin.

## DIALECT EVOLUTION IN GRIFFIN

A timeline of dialect change throughout the history of the American South would gravitate around political and economic events, such as wars and industrial advances. Bailey et al. (1996) characterize such events as "catastrophic" when they affect the trajectory of linguistic evolution. In the aftermath of an event such as World War II, for instance, migration patterns and the ecology of linguistic communities were altered. In Texas, Bailey et al. find that older linguistic features decline, are maintained, or expand due to factors that include local identity and adoption of features by newcomers. Also, internal processes of innovation and overgeneralization play a role (Tillery, Wikle, and Bailey 2000). At this level of usage, the feature signifies beyond its acknowledged parameters into the meaning-making realm of individual and group identity.

The events that shaped the evolution of English dialects in Griffin include wars, agricultural blights, and industrial shifts (see appendix B). The resultant changes in migration and social networks in turn effected mutated linguistic ecologies. New balances were struck on axes of identity and power that altered the configurations of occupation and even transformed family structures through "intermarriages."

At the same time, the regional patterns identified by dialectologists in the early twentieth century played important roles as founder varieties. To piece these components together in a rudimentary way is not very difficult: older features of South Midland varieties (such as *a*-verb-*ing*, plural verbal *-s*, and intrusive /r/) most likely formed the basis of mill-villager speech, since the founding mill villagers were largely coming from other mill villages and from Appalachia. Likewise, the older features established by the dialectologists as the Lowland Southern variety (such as lack of /r/ constriction and upgliding /ɔ/) probably formed the basis of farmer speech in the plantation belt of the South during the frontier era. Thus, the older generations represented in this study indicate that these two speech communities formed two communal dialects that existed side by side before World War II.

Later changes can also be regionalized (*y'all* and double modals in the Lowland South and fronted /au/ in the Appalachians, for example), but the picture already becomes fuzzy by the end of the World War II era, after which the middle generations reveal vigorous changes. The failure of agriculture and the concomitant expansion of the mill industry increased contact between the two formerly separate communities. This took place in different contexts: (1) at work, with farmers moving to the mills from the outlying areas; (2) in the schools, with more children attending school beyond the seventh grade in the consolidated high school;

and (3) socially, with people dating and even intermarrying. While older features began to decline during the period before World War II, vowel changes related to the "Southern Shift" began to expand in a "broad regional pattern" that encompasses the coastal southeast, the Appalachians, and the Piedmont (Labov 1997).

The most recent features to emerge, including several vowel mergers, vowel shifts, and monophthongization of /ay/, have not been clearly related to specific regional patterns. The younger generations in Griffin reflect the dispersion of both communities. Mill villages were sold off, and then in the 1980s textiles started to move overseas. At the same time that textile mills were closing, the city of Atlanta was growing and expanding, and Griffin is becoming a "bedroom community" at the time of this writing. While younger speakers are not necessarily conforming to a prescriptive norm, there are indications that their speech approximates a "Southern" norm that anchors their identity as noncity folk.

This swath of Georgia has long been a transition area due to its characteristics as an early frontier and as a transportation center. With the decline of textiles, Griffin has diversified and recently contributed to this transitional pattern, but its early history was one that preserved distinctions through the structuring power of occupational institutions that have often been likened to a feudal state.

McDAVID'S MILL TOWN. From his purview as a linguistic geographer and native of Greenville, South Carolina, a cotton mill town, Raven I. McDavid, Jr., noted several developments in the post–World War II era. Before this time, "every focal community lay in the plantation area; plantation families that prospered with the plantations set the prestige patterns" (1970, 58). However, with the rise of industry and urbanization, and tempered by improvements in education, the South Midland dialect began to wield more influence than plantation speech. The distribution of *r*-lessness, which is "part regional and part social" (53), declined in favor of South Midland /r/-constriction, but intrusive /r/, probably due to the influence of education, did not spread. McDavid found Upland vowels in Savannah speech, loss of distinctions between *horse/hoarse* and *merry/marry/Mary* in Knoxville, and Upland loss of glide in *tube, due,* and *new* by younger speakers in the Southern region. Some distinctions remained. For example, "below the Fall Line,"[1] speakers still pronounced the first vowel in *budget, bulge,* and *bulk* the same as the vowel in *cut* whereas speakers in the upper South maintained pronunciation of this vowel as the vowel in *put* (75). The South Midland variety, however, seemed to be winning out as early as 1948: Low Country *date* and *boat* [deət, boət] was receding in favor of Upland [deɪt, bout] (1948, 14, n. 27), initial /h-/ in *wheelbarrow* and *why* rarely occurred outside coastal centers, and vocabulary, such as *a little piece* ('a short distance') spread from Upland varieties to Lowland varieties (11, n. 12). McDavid attributes this new pattern of linguistic dominance to increases in mobility and education that resulted from industrialization and urbanization in the South. The textile workers played a large role in many towns throughout the Carolinas, Georgia, and Alabama: "[they] altered the structure of urban society in such a way that through the educational opportunities of their children and grandchildren they would inevitably affect the patterns of local cultivated speech" (1970, 67–68).

## NETWORKS IN GRIFFIN

The class structure of Griffin is discernible only in broad strokes that merely delineate a "town" class of businessmen and landowners in relief against a larger canvas of people who are not financially advantaged. These lower and lower-middle classes are internally diverse according to complex intersections of occupation, heritage, and race that can be intricately described through a social network approach. This type of analysis focuses on the consensus-based microlevel of social network ties that exist within a conflict-based macrolevel of social class (Milroy and Milroy 1992).

It might seem that the concept of prestige would be useful in this setting, but in actuality it would be very difficult to identify clear lines of preference and legitimacy, especially at this point at the beginning of the twenty-first century when social class and even occupation have intertwined in such convoluted ways. Prestige in itself is problematic for several reasons. The first immediate problem is that as soon as ethnographers identify a legitimate "prestige" variety, they invariably discover an equally robust counterpart, often labeled "covert prestige." This concept is redundant, oxymoronic, and generally circular in sociolinguistic studies. If a "covert" variety is actually a "prestige" variety, the legitimate (noncovert) prestige variety then is NOT a prestige variety for that speech community. Also, analyses that employ concepts of prestige tend to be monolithic in that they assume that each variety is representative of a semiotic process as a whole. The next step in such studies is to iron out the complexities of why certain members of a linguistic community use overt prestige varieties and others use covert ones. This in turn implies that overt prestige and covert prestige exist due to conflict-based microstructures. The idea of a "prestige" requires consensus of a community, but the very notion of "covert prestige" implies conflict (Milroy and Milroy 1992, 8). Prestige is always relative to a group.

Instead of applying the notion of prestige to linguistic and cultural differences in Griffin, the changing structure of network ties was examined to determine the routes of linguistic negotiation.

CLOSE-KNIT AND LOOSE-KNIT NETWORKS. Griffin, in the early decades of the twentieth century, embodied the seemingly endless postbellum struggle for independence. In a region of cash-crop agriculture, the semisubsistence farmer began to disappear. Depressions, along with natural blights, turned the small farm into an especially difficult means of making a living. Simultaneously, the textile mills expanded and offered a relatively safe haven for families. The setup of the mill villages instantiated what Giddens has described as "the reproduction of institutional practices" in day-to-day interactions (in Milroy and Milroy 1992, 2). The resultant network was dense and multiplex and existed in stark contrast to the loose-knit and eroding structures of small family farms. The mill workers were also psychologically counterpoised to the small farmer. In essence, both had sought means to support their families and provide opportunities for their children, but the routes they chose appeared to be oppositional. While the small farmer struggled increasingly with day-to-day survival, the mill village was such a paternalistic structure that the goal of independence seemed to have been subverted. Some mill owners were even characterized as carpetbaggers.[2] However, as in Marxist applications to language that identify dialect variation as "a form of social and cultural capital that is convertible into economic capital" (Milroy and Milroy 1992, 4), the mill villagers maintained a dialect informed by the founder population. Compounded by a heritage of social and linguistic isolation, the mill villagers' position as close-knit workers in a domineering institutional structure enabled cultural differentiation to be strongly expressed linguistically.

Close-knit networks tend to be conservative and are often quite successful in maintaining nonstandard forms. "Their capacity to do this, however, seems to be dependent on their territorial restriction to specific neighborhoods, the day-to-day behavior of individuals being less constrained by geographically dispersed networks" (Milroy and Milroy 1992, 6). The mill villagers accordingly maintained strong ties with each other that overlapped in neighborhoods, occupation, religion, school, socializing, and family. The characterization of the mill village community as being "just like a family" is as literal as it is metaphorical. Jobs were handed down throughout generations; coworkers and neighbors married; and extended families remained in the same small villages. Originally, farmers in the Griffin area also had close-knit communities in which families shared and divided up tracts of land. Farm children grew up in rural communities with their cousins, their grandparents, and often African American tenant farmers, but the declining farm economy diminished the close-knit character of the rural communities and rural workers increasingly moved into other occupations, often into the mills.

WEAK AND STRONG NETWORK TIES. The mill villagers, in their previous stage of social isolation, maintained a dialect constrained by socioeconomic parameters. The farmers, on the other hand, always had had access to a larger pool of features from a range of southern varieties, including African American vernaculars. This situation parallels Milroy and Milroy's interpretation of Philadelphia data presented by Labov and Harris (1986) and Ash and Myhill (1986). That study focused on two groups that negotiated features reflective of racial identification. Patterns of Blacks who used "White" forms and Whites who used "Black" forms were interpreted in terms of prestige and dominance. Milroy and Milroy analyze these patterns in terms of accommodation and weak ties: the White-oriented Blacks (WBs) who used White forms were not innovators—they had always had these forms present in the pool of features they selected from—whereas the Black-oriented Whites (BWs) were innovators—they did not always have the Black alternates in their range of variables. Thus, the BWs were accommodating. The parallel in Griffin centers on migration and settlement patterns. Farmers settled the land earlier when Georgia was the frontier. The diversity of backgrounds included Scotch-Irish, German, south and southwest English, and descendants of African slaves. Though they may have originated from tight-knit "cousinages," their community structure gradually became loose knit. Family ties remained dense and multiplex, but farmer families also attended elementary schools and churches with town folk. Even their neighborhoods were loose knit: older farmer Flora recalls seeing family every day, but the neighbors down the road only once or twice a month. Mike (from the middle-aged farm group) and Sam took turns walking home from school to Sam's house in town and the long haul to Mike's (more adventurous) house in the country. The mill villagers' background, on the other hand, stemmed primarily from the borderlands of the British Isles and followed migration routes of relative isolation in several locales (Europe, the Appalachians, mill villages). And the strong ties of this close-knit network continue. The two youngest informants of the Griffin sample, for instance, are the married couple Deena and Steve, both from the Highland mill village. Therefore, the pool of features that mill villagers selected from did not have the same variables that the other residents of Griffin did. Any subsequent changes in their dialect were thus accommodations to variables that were new to them. This scenario also accounts for the relatively conservative character of mill-villager speech; the isolate pattern was the founder pattern, and the close-knit network reinforced norm maintenance. Furthermore, changes in either sphere would, according to Milroy and Milroy, happen through weak ties (15), which the farmers had more of. In the Philadelphia studies, for example, the WBs who used White forms more often than the core Black population were "classic weak-tie type[s]"—con men who practiced on White people, not people who they knew well through strong network ties.

The weak-tie innovators in Griffin were the children of farmers who had contact with the children of mill workers (the middle-aged group). These contacts did not happen until high school or until they entered the workforce in the textile industries. The two high schools in Griffin[3] were not consolidated until the 1950s (and desegregation did not occur until the early 1970s). Earlier, many farmers and mill workers began their working life after graduating from the seventh grade, further narrowing the portion of the communities that would engage in contact with outsiders by attending high school. The farmers who turned to the textile industry for work often did not do so until after high school, and thus they entered the workforce at higher levels separate from the mill villagers who had grown up in the mills and taken on jobs handed down by relatives or neighbors. Farmers also rarely lived in the tight-knit mill villages; rather, they found transportation to the mills from their homes where some of them still farmed part-time. Farmers, then, gradually adapted to the New South economy and began to constitute a more loose-knit middle class in which weak ties abounded through religious, social, and educational venues and workplaces. Out of economic necessity, many farmers were moving into the middle class. Table 5.1 offers a simple adaptation of Milroy and Milroy's outline of typical patterns of maintenance and innovation through strong and weak network ties.

LIFE MODES. As Milroy and Milroy (1992, 9, 17) note, strong ties lead to local cohesion but overall fragmentation. Citing Højrup's (1983) concept of life modes, they describe how economic processes are reproduced in the day-to-day lives of individuals who make up clusters that are more accurately indexed to institutional structures than to traditional constructs of social class. However, life modes do correlate with network strength, which in turn makes up the broader level of social class and confirms that innovation often occurs in the middle class (19–22). Life modes are also helpful in assessing how institutions can enforce inequalities and conflict (19). The gaps between mill villagers and the other groups in

TABLE 5.2
Network Maintenance and Innovation Patterns Based on Strong and Weak Ties (adapted from Milroy and Milroy 1992)

| | *Internal Contacts* | *External Contacts* |
|---|---|---|
| Lower-class clusters | strong | weak |
| Middle-class clusters[a] | weak | weak |
| Upper-class clusters | strong | weak |

a. Middle-class clusters with weak ties both internally and externally tend to be linguistic innovators.

Griffin have not significantly decreased; even with the breakdown of the mills themselves, their hegemonic influences endure. This bifurcation of the lower-middle class parallels the description in Hojrup and Milroy and Milroy (see adaptation in fig. 5.1). In this framework, both mill villagers and farmers are splitting off in varying forms of Life Mode 2, which is a complex transitional stage. These wage earners differ from the self-employed in Life Mode 1, which is based on the family as a production unit, is necessarily close knit, and has the gaining of independence as its goal. In Griffin, the farmers once were self-employed, leading an existence as in Life Mode 1. However, only one family in the Griffin sample still farms as their sole means of employment. All the others have entered into other areas, either as "relatively affluent" wage earners as in Life Mode 2 or as managerial employees as in Life Mode 3. Mill villagers are still wage earners, usually "relatively poor" as described in Life Mode 2. The wage earner in Life Mode 2 has no control over the means of production in which they are incorporated. If wage levels rise significantly, however, a disintegration of the solidarity gained from neighborhood and trade unions is likely to occur in favor of economic and cultural opportunities. The cultural divide is further emphasized by the clear resentment that workers harbor against supervisors, who benefited from education but little "real" training. Zelda, for example, complains about the changes:

And then later, see, they had little inspectors ... that come round to your table and get in your work and look in it and see what was in it. They began—after them engineers come in there they hired just hired so many

FIGURE 5.1
Macro- and Microlevels of Sociolinguistic Structure
(from Milroy and Milroy 1992, [page #])

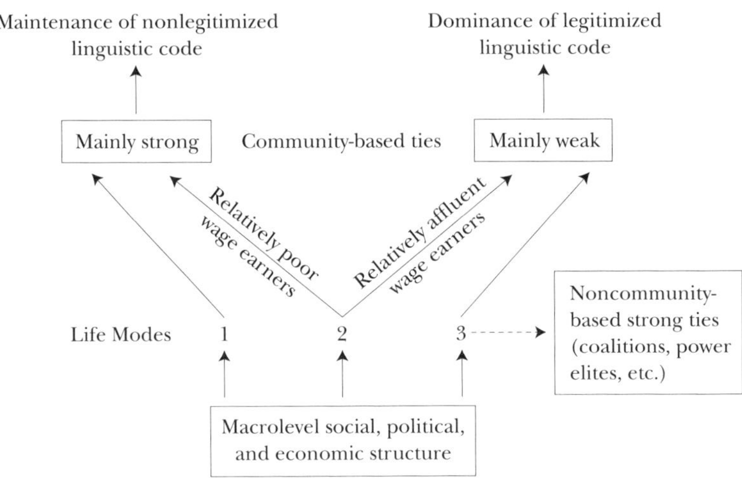


different ones to go round and look at people's work and that's that's one thing that ruined the bleachery.

Still, there are several mill villagers who risked social tension to earn higher paychecks in supervisory positions (such as the "little inspectors"). The fact that these slightly higher positions were often casualties of company restructuring only adds to the loose-knit character of this lower-middle class.

MOBILITY. These "contradictory modes of access to material and cultural domination" are dramatically played out in the different occupational roles in Griffin (Gal 1989). Mill villagers had an initial advantage in getting mill jobs through contacts that went back several generations. They also had first dibs on housing within the villages, and this access granted them the benefits of local schooling and a stable community. However, the farmers increasingly released their allegiance to agriculture and encouraged their children to gain a high school education, which would result in increased mobility—some of it upward mobility (especially in the form of managerial positions at the mills), some of it simply OUTWARD mobility. (Griffin is one of those towns that many teenagers can't wait to escape.) Mill villagers also gained mobility through increased education, though this development occurred at a slower pace than for farmers (who had been disfranchised earlier). Also, mill villagers still maintained tight-knit networks even as they gained mobility. This directed much of the mobility back homeward. In fact, sometimes the mill would pay for a college education if the recipients agreed to come back and apply their expertise in the mills. By the 1950s, many farmers were forced to become more outwardly mobile when considering their choice of work, while mill villagers often still followed family lines into the mills. Thus, the trajectory of economic processes and networks, and therefore dialect maintenance, are inextricably intertwined.

NETWORK SCALES IN GRIFFIN. Individual speakers in Griffin were scored for network density and multiplexity. Density correlates to Blom and Gumperz's (1972) notion of open versus closed communities; in a high-density, or closed, community, most members know each other and interact primarily within the community. These types of language communities tend to maintain low status or nonstandard dialects more than open communities in which members interact outside the territory with members of other communities (Milroy 1980, 20). Multiplexity refers to the number of different types of contact; for instance, multiplex speakers interact in several modes, such as work, friendship, neighborhood, and kin versus a uniplex relationship that depends solely on one type of interaction. When members of a community work, live, and marry together, the norm enforcement role of the community is usually quite strong. Table 5.2 displays the criteria for tabulating speakers' network scores. One point is assigned to each speaker for each criterion that he or she fulfills. A half-point is assigned to categories that were fulfilled in only one phase of life. For instance, many farmers grew up working on the farm with their families, but then had to leave to find gainful employment in their twenties.

Table 5.3 makes it abundantly clear that mill villagers have higher network scores, indicating that they have maintained strong

TABLE 5.2
Network Scale

DENSITY

1. Residence in a high-density cluster that is contralized around one mode of economic production.

MULTIPLEXITY

2. Working at the same place as at least two other family members and as at least the second generation of workers.
3. Residence in same cluster as at least two family members outside nuclear family structure.
4. Working at the same place as at least two others from the same area.
5. Voluntary association with workmates in leisure hours.

ties within the mill community. This is even true of the younger speakers. On the other hand, the farm speakers are part of a loose-knit community that consists mainly of weak ties to work, friends, and family. Communication networks are "points from which changes spread ... through the spontaneous communicative acts of individual speakers" (Mufwene 2001, 26). Certain speakers in this collection stand out according to their linguistic selections and their contact with others. Louise, for instance, grew up in a relatively tight-knit farm setting in which she lived, played, and worked with family who had lived on the same land for five generations. She did not leave home until her late 30s, instead staying at home to care for her parents and grandmother. When she did marry, she married a man from a poor family that had moved from job to job (sometimes in the mills) as he was growing up in Georgia. Since her teenage years, she also had close contact with Alice, a woman from the bleachery village who was Louise's uncle's second wife. Louise's pronunciation of /r/ departs from the average for her age group and occupational category, but approximates the nationwide norm and average for mill speech. She follows the lowland pattern for /ay/-monophthongization by maintaining a glide before voiceless environments 72% of the time. Her speech shows only moderate participation in the Back Shift, but vigorous participation in older, Lowland features associated with the Front Shift, the *pen-pin* merger, and the use of upgliding /aw/, which is resistant to

TABLE 5.3
Network Scores of Griffin Speakers

| | *Sex* | *Birthdate* | *Density* | *Multiplexity* | *Network Score* |
|---|---|---|---|---|---|
| Mill Villagers | | | | | |
| Patty | F | 1898 | 1 | 1-1-1-1 | 5 |
| Alice | F | 1913 | 1 | 1-1-1-1 | 5 |
| Zelda | F | 1921 | 1 | 1-1-1-1 | 5 |
| Alfred | M | 1904 | 1 | 1-1-1-1 | 5 |
| Paul | M | 1917 | 1 | 1-1-1-1 | 5 |
| Louis | M | 1911 | 1 | 1-1-1-1 | 5 |
| Rosa | F | 1949 | 1 | 1-1-1-1 | 5 |
| Janice | F | 1951 | 1 | 0-1-1-1 | 4 |
| Annie | F | 1943 | 0 | 0-1-1-1 | 3 |
| Gerald | M | 1946 | 0 | 1-1-1-1 | 4 |
| Larry | M | 1945 | 0 | 1-1-1-1 | 4 |
| David | M | 1950 | 1 | 1-1-1-1 | 5 |
| Jenny | F | 1969 | 0 | 1-1-1-1 | 4 |
| Kelly | F | 1972 | 1 | 1-1-1-1 | 5 |
| Deena | F | 1982 | 1 | 1-1-1-1 | 5 |
| Billy | M | 1969 | 1 | 1-1-1-1 | 5 |
| Steve | M | 1981 | 1 | 1-1-1-1 | 5 |
| Jason | M | 1970 | 0 | 0-1-1-1 | 3 |
| Farmers | | | | | |
| Flora | F | 1918 | 0 | .5-1-0-.5 | 2 |
| Helen | F | 1905 | 0 | .5-0-0-0 | .5 |
| Verna | F | 1918 | 0 | 1-1-0-0 | 2 |
| Robert | M | 1907 | 0 | .5-.5-0-.5 | 1.5 |
| Edward | M | 1910 | 0 | .5-.5-.0-.5 | 1.5 |
| Bob | M | 1914 | 0 | 1-0-1-0 | 2 |
| Lucille | F | 1942 | 0 | .5-.5-.5-0 | 1.5 |
| Louise | F | 1947 | 0 | .5-.5-.5-1 | 2.5 |
| Donna | F | 1944 | 0 | .5-0-0-0 | .5 |
| William | M | 1944 | 0 | .5-.5-.5-0 | 1.5 |
| John | M | 1948 | 0 | .5-.5-.5-0 | 1.5 |
| Herbert | M | 1939 | 0 | .5-.5-0-.5 | 1.5 |
| Ashley | F | 1977 | 0 | .5-.5-.5-.5 | 2 |
| Beth | F | 1975 | 0 | 0-0-0-0 | 0 |
| Wendy | F | 1969 | 0 | 0-0-.5-.5 | 1 |
| Peter | M | 1976 | 0 | .5-.5-.5-.5 | 2 |
| Will | M | 1970 | 0 | 1-1-1-1 | 4 |
| Tom | M | 1982 | 0 | 0-0-0-0 | 0 |

FIGURE 5.2
Louise's Feature Selections, Compared to Middle-Age Averages

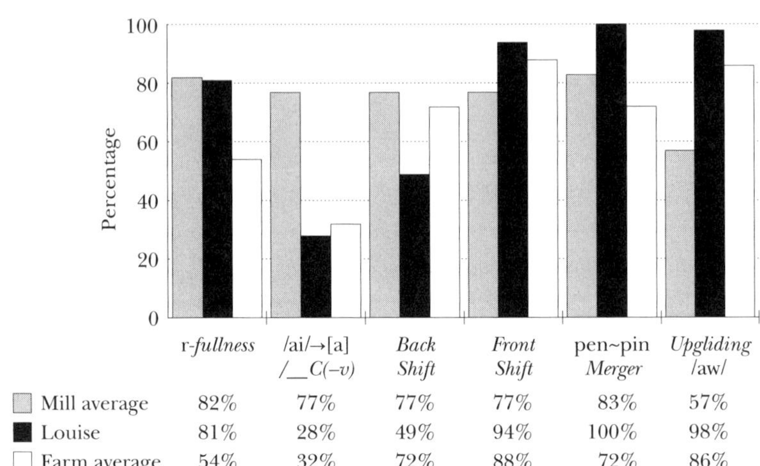


the *cot-caught* merger. Grammatically, she conforms to prescriptive nationwide standards, although she does employ *y'all*, *fixin to*, and *gonna*. Although many of her selections from the available pool of features do parallel the communal dialect of her occupational group and age range, her idiolect does not perfectly match. This is not surprising: it is to be expected that each individual speaker has a unique configuration that merely overlaps with other individual speakers' configurations. The communal dialect is the result of many individual acts.

On the other hand, many of Rosa's selections either match or surpass the communal dialect of mill villagers. In fact, she exemplifies the most robust pattern of the mill villagers' pattern for the shibboleths and the Southern Shift. As figure 5.3 shows, her speech is completely *r*-full, she monophthongizes in all environments, and participates in the Southern Shift. It appears that she is not participating as vigorously as Louise and Annie in the *pen-pin* merger, yet there is also no indication that she is maintaining the upgliding /aw/ that is resistant to the *cot-caught* merger. Although in most instances she does not merge /a/ and /aw/, by not choosing the upgliding /aw/ option she may be a precursor to the merger's

FIGURE 5.3
Rosa's Feature Selections, Compared to Middle-Age Averages

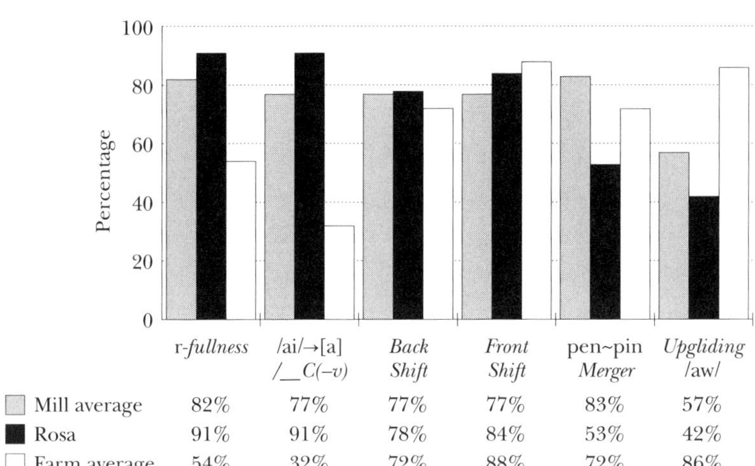


| | r-*fullness* | /ai/→[a] /__C(–v) | *Back Shift* | *Front Shift* | pen~pin *Merger* | *Upgliding* /aw/ |
|---|---|---|---|---|---|---|
| Mill average | 82% | 77% | 77% | 77% | 83% | 57% |
| Rosa | 91% | 91% | 78% | 84% | 53% | 42% |
| Farm average | 54% | 32% | 72% | 88% | 72% | 86% |

success. She also produces many instances of nonstandard subject-verb concord, perfective *done*, quasi-modals, *a*-verb-*ing*, and of course second-person plural *y'all*. Rosa still lives in the mill village where she grew up. Her husband works in the mill, and she also worked there until poor health prevented it. Her family, friends, and neighbors are all mill-folk.

A third speaker demonstrates a pattern of stereotypical mainstream "Southern." In figure 5.4, it is shown that Annie's speech is mostly *r*-full with some variation, and that /ay/-monophthongization is also variable, favoring the Lowland pattern of /a/ before voiceless and null environments but /ay/ before voiced environments. She also shows low to moderate approximation of the targets involved in the Southern Shift. She does not opt for the upgliding /aw/ that differentiates *cot* and *caught* for many Southern speakers. In fact, she is actually participating in the merger itself, with 28% of those tokens merged. Grammatically, she conforms to prescriptive norms, but regularly uses *y'all* and participates in the grammaticalization process of *fixin to* and *gonna*. It is noteworthy that Annie was born and raised in a mill village, then met and married William, a

FIGURE 5.4
Annie's Feature Selections, Compared to Middle-Age Averages

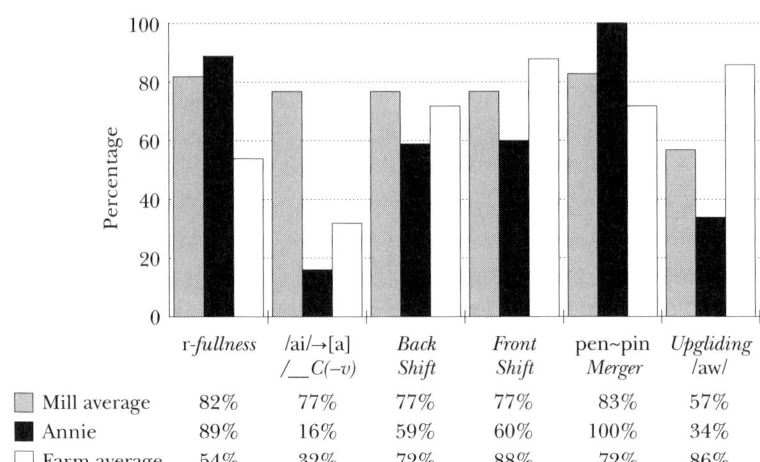


farmer. They currently live in Griffin near the mill village and take care of her mother.

These three speakers demonstrate that idiolects do not directly match the communal dialect but that contact between individuals is a prerequisite for linguistic evolution. Without contact, the available pool of features would not be heterogeneous. However, it is highly doubtful that a completely homogeneous reservoir has ever existed, since the very nature of language itself is communication between individual speakers, which involves multiple contributions (Mufwene 2001). The kinds of contact that happen in Griffin have changed over the past century. Louise's network score is 2.5, compared to Rosa's high score of 5 and Annie's average score of 3. Rosa's speech reflects strong ties in a close-knit network and therefore models conservative maintenance of the mill communal dialect. However, Louise and Annie have lower network scores, which reflect the fact that they have both fostered weak ties to other communities. They both "crossed over" in their marriages and yet both have maintained strong ties to their origins. Their speech models mutual accommodation that shows up in the younger generations, who are further expanding the available linguistic features through cultural dispersal that has resulted from the decline of both agriculture and centralized industry. Younger speakers, for instance, produce a mix that ranges from prescriptive-conscious speech (Tom, who now attends Georgia Tech) to codes of solidarity (Kelly, who is raising her daughter in East Griffin near her old mill neighborhood).

## CONCLUSION

I hope to have demonstrated some ways in which the combination of internal and external ecologies plays an important role in the development of new varieties of white English since the seventeenth century. In a system where both inherent variation and contact variation are the norm—that is, in all language change—it is not reasonable to expect language to change uniformly. As individual speakers engage in contact between communities, alternative strategies and unique selections from a pool of competing features take place. The successful features are not necessarily those that "improve" a dialect, but rather the features that are used by people in certain kinds of contact. The mill/farm occupational distinction in Griffin remained a cultural distinction for several generations, but economics and population shifts did not permit this type of contact to remain stable. As speakers of different communal dialects engaged in contact, they disassembled and re-created another communal dialect, formed by idiolectal choices from the new and expanded feature pool. As Griffin adjusts to future socioeconomic shifts, in which boundaries may not be so clearly drawn, individual speakers will continue to accommodate and maintain their dialects as they overlap and collaborate with other speakers.

# APPENDIXES

## A. VARIOUS PHONETIC NOTATIONS

| *Lexical Representation* | *Bailey* | *Feagin* | *Fridland* | *Labov* | *McNair* |
|---|---|---|---|---|---|
| *bait* | /e/ | /ey/ | /ey/ | /ey/ | /ey/ |
| *beat* | /i/ | /iy/ | /iy/ | /iy/ | /iy/ |
| *bet* | /ɛ/ | /e/ | /E/ | /e/ | /ɛ/ |
| *bit* | /ɪ/ | /i/ | /I/ | /i/ | /ɪ/ |
| *bat* | /æ/ | /ae/ | /æ/ | /æ/ | /æ/ |
| *boot* | /u/ | /uw/ | /uw/ | /uw/ | /uw/ |
| *book* | /ʊ/ | /U/ | /U/ | /u/ | /ʊ/ |
| *boat* | /o/ | /ow/ | /ow/ | /ow/ | /ow/ |
| *hawk* | /ɔ/ | /ɔw/ | /ɔ/ | /oh/ | /ɔ/ |
| *hock* | /ɑ/ | /ɔ/ | /ɑ/ | /o/ | /ɑ/ |
| *but* | /ʌ/ | /ʌ/ | /ʌ/ | /ʌ/ | /ʌ/ |
| *cow* | /au/ | /aw/ | /aw/ | /aw/ | /au/ |
| *tide* | /ai/ | /ay/ | /ay/ | /ay/ | /ay/ |

## B. ETHNOGRAPHIC TIMELINE FOR THE SOUTHEASTERN UNITED STATES AND GRIFFIN, GEORGIA

PERIOD BEFORE 1875

1600–1700 50,000 convicted criminals imported to colonies, primarily Virginia and Maryland (Bailyn 1988, 121)

1630 Indentured servants migrate to tobacco colonies (Bailyn 1988, 27)

1680 Blacks begin to outnumber whites in the labor force in a few of the tobacco colonies (Bailyn 1988, 28)

1709–10 Large migration of Germans to British territory—which scattered to Ireland and New York (Bailyn 1988, 33)

1733 Georgia founded by Oglethorpe as a nonslave province

1745 Destruction of Highlander clans and suppression of Jacobite rebellion—causes dislocation to Lowlands and to America (Bailyn 1988, 30)

1749 Slavery becomes legal in Georgia

1773 Weavers strike for higher wages in Paisley, Scotland, and succeed when they threaten to move "in a block" to America (Bailyn 1988, 38)

1763–76 Scotch-Irish emigration and the expansion of Georgia (Bailyn 1988, 147)

1776 Revolutionary War

Jan. 1821 Chief McIntosh ceded to the United States all land lying between the Flint and Ocmulgee rivers and north to the Chattahoochee River

1830 Griffin area parceled out in land lottery, during cotton boom

June 1840 Griffin founded by and named after General Lewis Lawrence Griffin. First acre sold for $1,000.

Dec. 1842 Griffin incorporated (http://www.spaldingcounty.com)

1843 Year of depression that bankrupted Gen. Griffin's Monroe Railroad, which was redirected to cross in Terminus (Atlanta) instead

1850 Compromise of 1850 postpones Civil War for a decade

Dec. 1851 Spalding County founded (named for Ed Spalding of Frederica on St. Simon's Island, Ga.)

1865 Civil War—Griffin not battle site, served as site of mobilization and hospital town. Railroad tracks that supported Griffin's economy destroyed by Union Gen. James Wilson.

1877 First appearance of "Jim Crow" laws in Georgia

PERIOD BETWEEN 1875 AND 1945

1888 Kinkaid Manufacturing Company constructed

1888 University of Georgia Experiment Station established in Griffin

1900 South has 4.5 million spindles (23% of national total) (Cash 1941, 216)

1903 Dr. Alexander McKelway, Southern secretary for the National Child Labor Committee, begins to wage war against industry for enactment of child labor laws (Cash 1941, 223)

1910 South has 11 million spindles (39% of national total) (Cash 1941, 216)

1903–25 Towels sent to Pennsylvania or Lowell, Mass., to be bleached and finished; Lowell Bleachery South constructed in 1925 in Griffin for onsite finishing early 1920s Extensive farm worker dislocation caused by the boll weevil

Jan. 1924 John H. Cheatham's Georgia Cotton merges with Kinkaid to form Georgia-Kinkaid Mills (Dundee)

1914–18 World War I—U.S. involvement begins in 1917. The Great War increases demand, which results in wage hikes and expansion of textile plants in the South. Postwar changes send industry into a tailspin, which results in plant closings and wage cuts (Hall et al. 1987, 183).

Jan. 1925 Construction begins on Crompton-Highland Mills

Oct. 1929 Stock Market crashes

Aug. 1932 Highland Mill and Gresham Manufacturing operating at 100%; Kinkaid and Rushton Mills operating at 65%

Sept. 1934 Highland Mill temporarily forced to close by union strikers

1938 Fair Labor Standards Act outlawed employment of children under sixteen (Hall et al. 1987, 60)

Dec. 7, 1941 Japanese attack Pearl Harbor

June 1941 American Mills (Griffin) experiments with DuPont's nylon hosiery pursuant to embargo on Japanese silk

1942–45 World War II—mill production directed toward war efforts; women go to work in the mills; many African Americans join military or move to northern industrial sites; soldiers come home to new economic landscape

PERIOD BETWEEN 1945 AND 2000

1954–65 Civil Rights Era

1971 Dundee acquires Colorcraft, creates Georgia Screen Printers in Newnan

1972 Dundee acquires Chicopee Manufacturing Company's baby products line and creates Dundee's Baby Products Division

Apr. 1976 Dundee acquires Georgia Schiffli Company in Manchester, Ga. (embroidered towels)

Aug. 1976 Dundee acquires Rushton plant in Griffin

July 1981 Dundee acquires Hampton Mills plant in Ellijay, Ga. (bath rugs)

Nov. 1982 Highland Mill closes

June 1990 Dundee acquires Hartwell Mills of Hartwell, Ga.

1996 Springs acquires Dundee

1999 Rushton plant closes

2001 Edton mill massive layoffs

# NOTES

## CHAPTER 1

1. A third dialect community, that of the African Americans, exists in Griffin but is discussed only in passing—when comparisons are warranted.

## CHAPTER 2

1. The government's plan to assist agriculture resulted in the unfortunate consequence of the government paying farmers to leave some fields uncultivated during a period when the market was glutted and prices were down. The plantation owners quickly realized that it was more profitable to plow under their own section of the land and let the tenant farmers sell harvested product for the lower market price. Thus, the owners reaped more profit for less labor while the tenants labored more and reaped less. Since the government sent the assistance checks directly to the owners, the tenant farmers had no control over the situation. Eventually, the owners realized that they could hire wage earners to work the land and thus receive even more of the profit, further propelling the decline of tenancy and the migration of laborers toward industry. If one considers the plutocracy affiliations and backgrounds of Southern politicians of the era, it seems doubtful that this situation was entirely accidental.
2. This information was contained in the report of the National Emergency Council, Odum's *Southern Regions of the United States* (1936), and the U.S. Census Reports.
3. Hahn (1983) describes the "yeomanry" of the Upcountry and Plantation Belt as an early middle class and criticizes scholars for assuming that all farmers were either very rich or very poor. However, his chronicle centers on the years 1840–90, and he analyzes how ideological conflicts, along with worsening conditions, set the stage for a deteriorating farm economy in the twentieth century. Cash (1941) also notes the yeomen as middle class but as one exploited by the plantation system.
4. Very early on, before the end of the seventeenth century, these indentured servants included Africans (Mufwene 2000b, 6).

5. Vocalization refers to the substitution of the allophone [ə] in place of rhoticized /r/ (Pederson 1986–92); monophthongization collapses the two sounds heard in a diphthong, such as the vowel sequence in *ride*, into one sound. This glide elimination, or perhaps glide assimilation, is not mere deletion, since it preserves length in the nucleus.

## CHAPTER 3

1. Appendix A lists the varying notations used by four of the current principal investigators of the Southern Shift.

## CHAPTER 5

1. The *Columbia Electronic Encyclopedia* defines *fall line* as a "boundary between an upland region and a coastal plain across which rivers from the upland region drop to the plain as falls or rapids. A fall line is formed in an area where the rivers have eroded away the soft rocks of a coastal plain more quickly than the older harder rocks of an upland region. Such erosion follows a crooked line along a coast. River vessels usually cannot travel beyond a fall line and their cargoes must be unloaded there. The falls . . . also supply water power for the development of industry such as textile and grist mills. For these reasons a fall line often marks a string of developed areas, such as the break between the Appalachian rise and the coastal plain of the eastern United States, where a band of commercial and industrial cities quickly developed in the nineteenth century, paralleling the line of port cities along the coasts. Typical fall-line cities on the Atlantic coast of the United States are Lowell, Mass.; Pawtucket, R.I.; Troy, N.Y.; Trenton, N.J.; Georgetown, now part of Washington, D.C.; Richmond, Va.; Raleigh, N.C.; Columbia, S.C.; and Augusta, Ga. Among the fall-line cities of the Mississippi valley are Fredville, Ky., and Minneapolis, Minn." (http://www.encyclopedia.com/articlesnew/04360.html).
2. According to *Merriam-Webster's Collegiate Dictionary* (2003), *carpetbagger* dates back to 1868 and is defined as "a Northerner in the South after the American Civil War usually seeking private gain under the reconstruction governments," the term having come from "their carrying all their belongings in carpetbags."
3. The two high schools were on separate sides of town that mainly catered to mill students versus town and farm students. Black and white schools were not integrated until 1969.

# REFERENCES


Agee, James, and Walker Evans. 1941. *Let Us Now Praise Famous Men: Three Tenant Families.* Boston: Houghton-Mifflin. Repr., 1988.

Ash, Sharon, and John Myhill. 1986. "Linguistic Correlates of Inter-Ethnic Contact." In *Diversity and Diachrony,* ed. David Sankoff, 33–44. Amsterdam: Benjamins.

Atwood, E. Bagby. 1953. *A Survey of Verb Forms in the Eastern United States.* Ann Arbor: Univ. of Michigan Press.

Aucoin, Michelle. 1997. "Grammaticization and Analogy in the Development of Future Tense Markers in AAVE." Poster presented at the annual meeting on New Ways of Analyzing Variation (NWAVE 26), Quebec, Oct. 23–26.

Bailey, Guy. 1993. "A Perspective on African-American English." *American Dialect Research,* ed. Dennis R. Preston, 287–318. Amsterdam: Benjamins.

———. 1997. "When Did Southern American English Begin?" In *Englishes around the World: Studies in Honour of Manfred Görlach,* vol. 1, *General Studies, British Isles, North America,* ed. Edgar W. Schneider, 255–75. Amsterdam: Benjamins.

Bailey, Guy, and Natalie Maynor. 1989. "The Divergence Controversy." *American Speech* 64: 12–39.

Bailey, Guy, and Jan Tillery. 1996. "The Persistence of Southern American English." *Journal of English Linguistics* 24: 308–21.

Bailey, Guy, Tom Wikle, Jan Tillery, and Lori Sand. 1993. "Some Patterns of Linguistic Diffusion." *Language Variation and Change* 5: 359–90.

———. 1996. "The Linguistic Consequences of Catastrophic Events: An Example from the American Southwest." In *Sociolinguistic Variation: Data, Theory, and Analysis; Selected Papers from NWAV23 at Stanford,* ed. Jennifer Arnold, Reneé Blake, Brad Davidson, Scott Schwenter, and Julie Solomon, 435–51. Stanford, Calif.: Center for the Study of Language and Information, Stanford Univ.

Bailyn, Bernard. 1988. *The Peopling of British North America: An Introduction.* New York: Vintage.

Bernstein, Cynthia, Thomas Nunnally, and Robin Sabino, eds. 1997. *Language Variety in the South Revisited.* Tuscaloosa: Univ. of Alabama Press.

Blom, Jan-Petter, and John J. Gumperz. 1972. "Social Meaning in Linguistic Structures: Code-Switching in Norway." In *Directions in Sociolinguistics,* ed. John J. Gumperz and Dell Hymes, 407–34. New York: Holt, Rinehart and Winston.

Brown, Vivian Ruby. 1990. "The Social and Linguistic History of a Merger: /ɪ/ and /ɛ/ before Nasals in Southern American English." Ph.D. diss., Texas A&M Univ.

———. 1991. "Evolution of the Merger of /ɪ/ and /ɛ/ before Nasals in Tennessee." *American Speech* 66: 303–15.

Butters, Ronald R. 1989. *The Death of Black English: Divergence and Convergence in Black and White Vernaculars.* Frankfurt am Main: Lang.

———. 1991. "Multiple Modals in United States Black English: Synchronic and Diachronic Aspects." In *Verb Phrase Patterns in Black English and Creole,* ed. Walter F. Edwards and Donald Winford, 165–76. Detroit, Mich.: Wayne State Univ. Press.

Caldwell, Erskine, and Margaret Bourke-White. 1937. *You Have Seen Their Faces.* New York: Modern Age Books. Repr., Athens: Univ. of Georgia Press, 1995.

Cash, W. J. 1935. "Two U.N.C. Professors Produce a Penetrating Social History." Rev. of *The South Looks at Its Past,* by Benjamin Burks Kendrick and Alex Mathews Arnett. *Charlotte News,* Dec. 8. http://wjcash.org/WJCash4/Charlotte.News.Articles/UNCProfessors.htm (accessed July 15, 2005).

———. 1938. "The No. One Problem: Roosevelt Looks to Odum." *Charlotte News,* July 17. http://www.wjcash.org/WJCash1/Charlotte.News.Articles/Odum.htm (accessed July 15, 2005).

———. 1941. *The Mind of the South.* New York: Knopf. Repr. New York: Vintage, 1991.

Ching, Marvin K. L. 1987. "How Fixed Is *fixin to?*" *American Speech* 62: 332–45.

Christian, Donna, Walt Wolfram, and Nanjo Dube. 1988. *Variation and Change in Geographically Isolated Communities: Appalachian English and Ozark English.* Publication of the American Dialect Society 74. Tuscaloosa: Univ. of Alabama Press.

*The Columbia Electronic Encyclopedia.* 2000. 6th ed. Columbia University Press. http://www.encyclopedia.com/articlesnew/04360.html.

Cram, Geo. F. 1897. "Cram's Railroad and County Map of Georgia." Hargrett Rare Book and Manuscript Library, Univ. of Georgia Libraries. http://www.libs.uga.edu/darchive/hargrett/maps/1879c6b.jpg (accessed July 15, 2002).

Cukor-Avila, Patricia. 1995. "The Evolution of AAVE in a Rural Texas Community: An Ethnolinguistic Study." Ph.D. diss., Univ. of Michigan.

Davis, Alva L., Raven I. McDavid, Jr., and Virginia G. McDavid, eds. 1969. *A Compilation of the Work Sheets of the Linguistic Atlas of the United States and Canada and Associated Projects.* 2nd ed. Chicago: Univ. of Chicago Press.

Dil, Anwar S., ed. 1980. *Varieties of American English: Essays.* Stanford, Calif.: Stanford Univ. Press.

Dillard, J. L. 1972. *Black English: Its History and Usage in the United States.* New York: Random House.

Di Paolo, Marianna. 1986. "A Study of Double Modals in Texas English." Ph.D. diss., Univ. of Texas at Austin.

Eckert, Penelope. 1989. "The Whole Woman: Sex and Gender Differences in Variation." *Language Variation and Change* 1: 245–67. Repr. in *The Matrix of Language: Contemporary Linguistic Anthropology*, ed. Donald Brenneis and Ronald Macaulay, 116–37. Boulder, Colo.: Westview, 1996.

Feagin, Crawford. 1979. *Variation and Change in Alabama English: A Sociolinguistic Study of the White Community.* Washington, D.C.: Georgetown Univ. Press.

———. 1986a. "Competing Norms in the White Speech of Anniston, Alabama." In *Language Variety in the South: Perspectives in Black and White*, ed. by Michael B. Montgomery and Guy Bailey, 216–34. University: Univ. of Alabama Press.

———. 1986b. "More Evidence for Major Vowel Change in the South." In *Diversity and Diachrony*, ed. David Sankoff, 83–95. Amsterdam: Benjamins.

———. 1990. "The Dynamics of a Sound Change in Southern States English: From *r*-less to *r*-full in Three Generations." In *Development and Diversity: Language Variation across Time and Space; A Festschrift for Charles-James N. Bailey*, ed. Jerold A. Edmondson, Crawford Feagin, and Peter Mühlhäusler, 129–46. Dallas, Tex.: Summer Institute of Linguistics.

———. 1994. "'Long *i*' as a Microcosm of Southern States Speech." Paper presented at the annual meeting on New Ways of Analyzing Variation in English (NWAVE 23), Stanford, Calif., Oct. 20–23.

———. 1997. "The African Connection to Southern States English." In Bernstein, Nunnally, and Sabino, 123–39.

———. 2000. "What's Happened to the Southern Shift?" Paper presented at the biannual SouthEastern Conference on Linguistics (SECOL 62), Oxford, Miss., Apr. 6–8.

Federal Writers' Project, Works Progress Administration. 1939. *These Are Our Lives.* Chapel Hill: Univ. of North Carolina Press.

Fischer, David Hackett. 1989. *Albion's Seed: Four British Folkways in America.* New York: Oxford Univ. Press.

Fridland, Valerie. 2000. "The Southern Shift in Memphis, Tennessee." *Language Variation and Change* 11: 267–85.

Gal, Susan. 1989. "Language and Political Economy." *Annual Review of Anthropology* 18: 345–67.

Gumperz, J. 1972. "The Speech Community." In *Language and Social Context: Selected Readings*, comp. Pier Paolo Giglioli, 219–31. Harmondsworth: Penguin.

Hahn, Steven. 1983. *The Roots of Southern Populism: Yeoman Farmers and the Transformation of the Georgia Upcountry, 1850–1890*. New York: Oxford Univ. Press.

Hall, Jacquelyn Dowd, James Leloudis, Robert Korstad, Mary Murphy, Lu-Ann Jones, and Christopher B. Daly. 1987. *Like a Family: The Making of a Southern Cotton Mill World*. Chapel Hill: Univ. of North Carolina Press.

Harris, Alice C. 1997. "Remarks on Grammaticalization." *Proceedings of the LFG '97 Conference*, ed. Miriam Butt and Tracy Holloway Kings. San Diego, Calif.: CSLI (Center for the Study of Language of Information) Publications. http://csli-publications.stanford.edu/LFG/2/harris-lfg97.html(accessed July 15, 2005).

Hazen, Kirk. 1996. "Dialect Affinity and Subject-Verb Concord: The Appalachian-Outer Banks Connection." *SECOL Review* 20: 25–53.

Herold, Ruth. 1990. "Mechanisms of Mergers: The Implementation and Distribution of the Low Back Merger in Eastern Pennsylvania." Ph.D. diss., Univ. of Pennsylvania.

Højrup, Thomas. 1983. "The Concept of Life-Mode: A Form-Specifying Mode of Analysis Applied to Contemporary Western Europe." *Ethnologia Scandinavica* 13: 15–50.

Horn, James. 1979. "Servant Emigration to the Chesapeake in the Seventeenth Century." In *The Chesapeake in the Seventeenth Century: Essays on Anglo-American Society*, ed. Thad W. Tate and David Ammerman, 51–95. Chapel Hill: Univ. of North Carolina Press.

Inter-university Consortium for Political and Social Research (ICPSR). 1998. "United States Historical Census Data Browser." http://fisher.lib.virginia.edu/census/ (accessed Jan. 13 2000).

Jespersen, Otto. 1954a. *A Modern English Grammar on Historical Principles*. Part 4, *Syntax*. London: Allen and Unwin.

———. 1954b. *A Modern English Grammar on Historical Principles*. Part 6, *Morphology*. London: Allen and Unwin.

Kemble, Frances Anne. 1961. *Journal of a Residence on a Georgian Plantation in 1838–1839*. Ed. John A. Scott. New York: Knopf. Repr., Athens: Univ. of Georgia Press, 1984.

Kerswill, Paul 2003. "Dialect Levelling and Geographical Diffusion in British English." In *Social Dialectology: In Honour of Peter Trudgill*, ed. David Britain and Jenny Cheshire, 223–43. Amsterdam: Benjamins.

Krapp, George Philip. 1925. *The English Language in America.* New York: Century.

Kretzschmar, William A., Jr. 1996. "Foundations of American English." In *Focus on the USA*, ed. Edgar W. Schneider, 25–50. Amsterdam: Benjamins.

Kurath, Hans. 1928. "The Origin of the Dialectal Differences in Spoken American English." *Modern Philology* 25: 385–95. Repr. in *A Various Language: Perspectives on American Dialects*, ed. Juanita V. Williamson and Virginia Burke, 12–21. New York: Holt, Rinehart and Winston, 1971.

———. 1940. "Dialect Areas, Settlement Areas, and Culture Areas in the United States." In *The Cultural Approach to History*, ed. Caroline F. Ware, 331–35. New York: Columbia Univ. Press.

———. 1949. *A Word Geography of the Eastern United States.* Ann Arbor: Univ. of Michigan Press.

Kurath, Hans, and Raven I. McDavid, Jr. 1961. *The Pronunciation of English in the Atlantic States: Based upon the Collections of the Linguistic Atlas of the Eastern United States.* Ann Arbor: Univ. of Michigan Press.

Labov, William. 1994. *Principals of Linguistic Change.* Vol. 1, *Internal Factors.* Oxford: Blackwell.

———. 1996. "The Organization of Dialect Diversity in North America." http://www.ling.upenn.edu/phono_atlas/ICSLP4.html (accessed July 15, 2005).

Labov, William, and Sharon Ash. 1997. "Understanding Birmingham." In Bernstein, Nunnally, and Sabino, 508–73.

Labov, William, Sharon Ash, and Charles Boberg. 1997. "A National Map of the Regional Dialects of American English." http://www.ling.upenn.edu/phono_atlas/home.html.

———. 2001. Introduction and chapter 18, "The South." *Atlas of North American English.* Online draft to be published by Mouton de Gruyter. http://www.ling.upenn.edu/phono_atlas/ANAE/ToC.html (accessed Mar. 30, 2001).

Labov, William, Paul Cohen, Clarence Robins, and John Lewis. 1968. *A Study of the Nonstandard English of Negro and Puerto Rican Speakers in New York City.* Office of Education, U.S. Department of Health, Education, and Welfare. Cooperative Research Project no. 3288. Philadelphia: U.S. Regional Survey.

Labov, William, and Wendell Harris. 1986. "De Facto Segregation of Black and White Vernaculars." In *Diversity and Diachrony*, ed. David Sankoff, 1–24. Amsterdam: Benjamins.

Labov, William, Malcah Yaeger, and Richard Steiner. 1972. *A Quantitative Study of Sound Change in Progress*. Philadelphia, Pa.: U.S. Regional Survey.

Lane, Lisa Ann. 2001. "Creating and Balancing Identities: (Re)Constructing Sociolinguistic Spaces through Dialect Change in Real Time." *Univ. of Pennsylvania Working Papers in Linguistics* 7.3: 145–58.

*Linguistic Atlas of the Gulf States*. 1986–92. Ed. Lee Pederson. 7 vols. Athens: Univ. of Georgia Press.

Lyons, John. 1968. *Introduction to Theoretical Linguistics*. London: Cambridge Univ. Press.

Macready, William Charles. 1912. *The Diaries of William Charles Macready*. Ed. William Toynbee. 2 vols. New York: Putnam.

McCullers, Carson. 1940. *The Heart Is a Lonely Hunter*. Boston: Houghton Mifflin. Repr., New York: Bantam, 1970.

McDavid, Raven I., Jr. 1948. "Postvocalic /-r/ in South Carolina: A Social Analysis." *American Speech* 23: 194–203. Repr. in Dil 1980, 1–14.

———. 1966. "Dialect Differences and Social Differences in an Urban Society." In *Sociolinguistics: Proceedings of the UCLA Sociolinguistics Conference 1964*, ed. William Bright, 72–83. The Hague: Mouton. Repr. in Dil 1980, 34–50.

———. 1970. "Changing Patterns of Southern Dialects." In *Essays in Honor of Claude M. Wise*, ed. Arthur J. Bronstein, Claude L. Shaver, and C. J. Stevens, 206–28. Hannibal, Mo.: Standard. Repr. in Dil 1980, 51–77.

———. 1975. "The Urbanization of American English." *Philologica Pragensia* 18: 228–38. Repr. in Dil 1980, 114–30.

McKinley, Judy Glanton. 1999. *A Southern Legacy: Life on a Mill Village*. Rocky Mount, Va.: Briarwood.

Meillet, Antoine. 1912. "L'évolution des formes grammaticales." *Scientia: Revista di scienza* 12: 384–400.

Melton, Quimby, Jr. 1996. *History of Griffin, Ga., 1840–1940*. Griffin, Ga.: Hometown.

Mencken, H. L. 1936. *The American Language: An Inquiry into the Development of English in the United States*. New York: Knopf.

*Merriam-Webster's Collegiate Dictionary*. 2003. 11th ed. Springfield, Mass.: Merriam-Webster.

Mille, Katherine Wyly. 1997. "Ambrose Gonzales' Gullah: What It May Tell Us about Variation." In Bernstein, Nunnally and Sabino, 98–112.

Milroy, James. 1992. *Language Variation and Change: On the Historical Sociolinguistics of English.* Oxford: Blackwell.

Milroy, Lesley. 1980. *Language and Social Networks.* Oxford: Blackwell.

———. 1987a. *Language and Social Networks.* 2nd ed. Oxford: Blackwell.

———. 1987b. *Observing and Analysing Natural Language: A Critical Account of Sociolinguistic Method.* Oxford: Blackwell.

———. 1992. "New Perspectives in the Analysis of Sex Differentiation in Language." In *Sociolinguistics Today: International Perspectives,* ed. Kingsley Bolton and Helen Kwok, 162–79. London: Routledge.

Milroy, Lesley, and James Milroy. 1992. "Social Network and Social Class: Toward an Integrated Sociolinguistic Model." *Language in Society* 21: 1–26.

Mishoe, Margaret, and Michael Montgomery. 1994. "The Pragmatics of Multiple Modal Variation in North and South Carolina." *American Speech* 69: 3–29.

Montgomery, Michael B. 1989. "English Language." In *Encyclopedia of Southern Culture,* ed. Charles Reagan Wilson and William Ferris, vol. 2, 609–20. New York: Anchor.

———. 1994a. "The Evolution of Verbal Concord in Scots." In *Studies in Scots and Gaelic: Proceedings of the Third International Conference on the Languages of Scotland,* ed. Alexander Fenton and Donald A. MacDonald, 81–95. Edinburgh: Canongate Academic.

———. 1994b. "Koinéization of Colonial American English." In *Proceedings of the Sixteenth Annual Meeting of the Atlantic Provinces Linguistic Association, University of Moncton, Moncton, New Brunswick, November 6–7, 1992,* ed. Catherine Phlipponneau et al., 309–31. Moncton, N.B.: Atlantic Provinces Linguistic Assn.

———. 1996a. "The Future of Southern American English." *SECOL Review* 20: 1–24.

———. 1996b. "Was Colonial American English a Koiné?" In *Speech Past and Present: Studies in English Dialectology in Memory of Ossi Ihalainen,* ed. Juhani Klemola, Merja Kytö, and Matti Rissanen, 213–35. Frankfurt am Main: Lang.

Montgomery, Michael B., and Guy Bailey, eds. 1986. *Language Variety in the South: Perspectives in Black and White.* University: Univ. of Alabama Press.

Mufwene, Salikoko S. 1996. "The Founder Principle in Creole Genesis." *Diachronica* 13: 83–134.

———. 1997. "The Ecology of Gullah's Survival." *American Speech* 72: 69–83.

———. 1998. "What Research on Creole Genesis Can Contribute to Historical Linguistics." In *Historical Linguistics, 1997: Selected Papers from the 13th International Conference on Historical Linguistics, Düsseldorf, 10–17 August 1997*, ed. Monika S. Schmid, Jennifer R. Austin, and Dieter Stein, 315–38. Amsterdam: Benjamins.

———. 1999. "North American Varieties of English as Byproducts of Population Contacts." In *The Workings of Language: From Prescriptions to Perspectives*, ed. Rebecca S. Wheeler, 15–37. Westport, Conn.: Praeger.

———. 2000a. "Population Contacts and the Evolution of English." *European English Messenger* 9: 9–15.

———. 2000b. "The Shared Ancestry of African-American and American White Southern Englishes: Some Speculations Dictated by History." Unpublished MS.

———. 2000c. "Some Sociohistorical Inferences about the Development of AAE." In *The English History of African American English*, ed. Shana Poplack, 233–63. Malden, Mass.: Blackwell.

———. 2001. *The Ecology of Language Evolution.* Cambridge: Cambridge Univ. Press.

Odum, Howard W. 1936. *Southern Regions of the United States.* Chapel Hill: Univ. of North Carolina Press.

Pederson, Lee, ed. 1986–92. *Linguistic Atlas of the Gulf States.* 7 vols. Athens: Univ. of Georgia Press.

Purdy, Geraldine, ed. 1983. *Abstracts of Deed Book A, Spalding County, 1952–1855.* Griffin, Ga.: Griffin Historical and Preservation Soc.

Roy, Donald F. 1965. "Change and Resistance to Change in the Southern Labor Movement." In *The South in Change and Continuity*, ed. John C. McKinney and Edgar T. Thompson, 225–47. Durham, N.C.: Duke University Press.

Said, Edward W. 1979. *Orientalism.* New York: Vintage.

Silverstein, Michael. 1998. "Contemporary Transformations of Local Linguistic Communities." *Annual Review of Anthropology* 27: 401–26.

Simpson, Richard L., and David R. Norsworthy. 1965. "The Changing Occupational Structure of the South." In *The South in Change and Continuity*, ed. John C. McKinney and Edgar T. Thompson, 198–224. Durham, N.C.: Duke University Press.

Stewart, William A. 1967. " Sociolinguistic Factors in the History of American Negro Dialects." *Florida FL Reporter* 5: 11.

Thomas, Erik, and Guy Bailey. 1992. "Competing Mergers and Their Resolution." *SECOL Review* 16: 179–200.

Tillery, Jan. 1989. "The Merger of the Phonemes /ɔ/ and /ɑ/ in Texas: A Study of Sociological and Phonetic Constraints." Master's thesis, Texas A&M Univ.

Tillery, Jan, Tom Wikle, and Guy Bailey. 2000. "The Nationalization of a Southernism." *Journal of English Linguistics* 28: 280–94.

Traugott, Elizabeth Closs. 1972. *A History of English Syntax: A Transformational Approach to the History of English Sentence Structure.* New York: Holt, Rinehart, and Wilston.

Trudgill, Peter. 1974. *The Social Differentiation of English in Norwich.* Cambridge: Cambridge Univ. Press.

Van Hoosier-Carey, Gregory. 1999. "Regional Accents, National Voices: English Studies, Postbellum Literature, and the Rearticulation of Southern Identity." http://www.lcc.gatech.edu/~gvanhoosier-carey/book.html (accessed Oct. 20, 2000).

Wolfram, Walt. 1993. "Identifying and Interpreting Variables." In *American Dialect Research,* ed. Dennis R. Preston, 193–222. Amsterdam: Benjamins.

Wolfram, Walt, and Donna Christian. 1976. *Appalachian Speech.* Arlington, Va.: Center for Applied Linguistics.

Wolfram, Walt, Kirk Hazen, and Natalie Schilling-Estes. 1999. *Dialect Change and Maintenance on the Outer Banks.* Publication of the American Dialect Society 81. Tuscaloosa: Univ. of Alabama Press.

Woodward, C. Vann. 1974. *The Strange Career of Jim Crow.* 3rd rev. ed. New York: Oxford Univ. Press.

Woofter, T. J., Jr. 1936. *Landlord and Tenant on the Cotton Plantation.* Works Progress Administration, Division of Social Research. Washington, D.C.: GPO.

Wright, Gavin. 1986. *Old South, New South: Revolutions in the Southern Economy since the Civil War.* New York: Basic Books.

Wright, Joseph, ed. 1898–1905. *The English Dialect Dictionary: Being the Complete Vocabulary of All Dialect Words Still in Use, or Known to Have Been in Use during the Last Two Hundred Years.* London: Frowde.